# TOP **10**
# MONTRÉAL
# & QUÉBEC CITY

## GREGORY B. GALLAGHER

EYEWITNESS TRAVEL

Left **Vieux-Port, Montréal** Right **Snowshoeing, Montréal**

LONDON, NEW YORK,
MELBOURNE, MUNICH AND DELHI
www.dk.com

Produced by Sargasso Media Ltd, London
Reproduced by Colourscan, SingaporePrinted and
bound by South ChinaPrinting Co. Ltd, China

First American Edition, 2004
10 11 12 13 10 9 8 7 6 5 4 3 2 1

Published in the United States by DK Publishing,
375 Hudson Street, New York,
New York 10014

**Reprinted with revisions 2006, 2008, 2010**

**Copyright 2004, 2010 ©
Dorling Kindersley Limited, London
A Penguin Company**

A catalog record of this book is available from the
Library of Congress.

ISSN 1479-344X
ISBN 9-780-7566-6087-1

Within each Top 10 list in this book, no hierarchy of
quality or popularity is implied. All 10 are, in the
editor's opinion, of roughly equal merit.

> **We're trying to be cleaner and greener:**
> - we recycle waste and switch things off
> - we use paper from responsibly managed
>   forests whenever possible
> - we ask our printers to actively reduce
>   water and energy consumption
> - we check out our suppliers' working
>   conditions – they never use child labour
>
> **Find out more about our values and
> best practices at www.dk.com**

# Contents

## Montréal & Québec City's Top 10

**The information in this DK Eyewitness Top 10 Travel Guide is checked regularly.**
Every effort has been made to ensure that this book is as up-to-date as possible at the time of
going to press. Some details, however, such as telephone numbers, opening hours, prices, gallery
hanging arrangements and travel information are liable to change. The publishers cannot accept
responsibility for any consequences arising from the use of this book, nor for any material on third party
websites, and cannot guarantee that any website address in this book will be a suitable source of travel
information. We value the views and suggestions of our readers very highly. Please write to:
Publisher, DK Eyewitness Travel Guides,
Dorling Kindersley, 80 Strand, London, Great Britain WC2R 0RL.

JACKET: Cover: Front – **DK Images**: Alan Keohane clb; **Photolibrary**: JTB Photo main. Spine – **DK Images**:
Demetrio Carrasco b. Back – **DK Images**: Demetrio Carrasco c, cr; Alan Keohane cl.

Left **Stade Olympique, Montréal** Right **Rue du Petit Champlain, Québec City**

Left **Basilique-Sainte-Anne-de-Beaupré** Right **Les Glissades, Québec City**

*Key to abbreviations*
**Adm** *admission charge* **Free** *no admission charge* **Dis. access** *disabled access*

# MONTRÉAL AND QUÉBEC CITY'S TOP 10

MONTRÉAL & QUÉBEC CITY'S TOP 10

# ᵀᴼᴾ10 Montréal and Québec City's Highlights

*Situated on the mighty St Lawrence River, the sights of these two cities captivate visitors with their history, culture and festivity. Not only were they both major players in the foundation of Canada but their portside locations have kept them at the heart of international commerce, resulting in a harmonious blend of heritage architecture and exciting modern venues that charm all those who come to Canada's "belle province."*

### Parc du Mont-Royal 1
Looming over Montréal's bustling activity, this mountain park is the most visited attraction in the city *(see pp8–11)*.

### Basilique Notre-Dame 2
North America's largest church when constructed in 1829 is still the Gothic Revival gem of Vieux-Montréal *(see pp12–13)*.

### Parc Olympique 3
Parc Olympique's many attractions include botanical gardens, an insectarium and sports facilities *(see pp14–17)*.

### Musée Pointe-à-Callière 4
The true birthplace of Montréal represents a merging of the city's past history and modern technology. Cutting-edge exhibitions and archeological artifacts allow visitors to experience six centuries of local life *(see pp18–19)*.

### Musée des Beaux-Arts de Montréal 5
The oldest and largest Québec museum contains works dating from antiquity to contemporary masters *(see pp20–21)*.

**Montréal**

1 Parc du Mont-Royal

5 Musée des Beaux Arts

Quartier Latin

Chinatown

Downtown

2 Basilique Notre-Dame

Vieux-Montréal

4 Musée Pointe-à-Callière

Vieux-Port

1000 yards — 0 — meters — 1000

### 6 La Citadelle, Québec City
Three centuries of military presence continue in this working army base, which is home to a hospital, officers' mess, and the first observatory in Canada *(see pp22–3)*.

Basilique 8 Sainte-Anne-de-Beaupré

Charlesbourg

9 Île d'Orléans

St-Raymond

6 7 Québec City

Ste-Thècle

Cap-Rouge

Charny

St-Titre

St-Casimir

Donnacona

St-Agapit

Ste-Marie

Trois-Rivières

Villeroy

Bécancour

East Broughton

Nicolet

Plessisville

St-Léonard-d'Aston

Thetford Mines

Victoriaville

Warwick

Disraeli

Drummondville

St-Nicéphore

Richmond

40 — miles — 0 — km — 40

### 7 Musée de la Civilisation de Québec
The MCQ's exhibits include artifacts from the First Nations, Chinese *objets d'art*, and items relating to everyday life in Québec during its 400-year history *(see pp24–5)*.

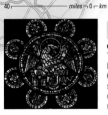

### 8 Basilique Sainte-Anne-de-Beaupré
This granite basilica, built between 1923–63, features 240 stained-glass windows and a gleaming mosaic *(see pp26–7)*.

### 9 Île d'Orléans
Known as the "cradle of French civilization in North America," this island of farm communities continues to preserve the traditions of the original settlers *(see pp28–9)*.

### 10 Les Laurentides
This mountain range has long been the favorite year-round playground for weekenders and vacationers with its pristine lakes, hiking trails and ski slopes *(see pp30–31)*.

# Parc du Mont-Royal

*The geographic highlight of Montréal are undeniably Mont-Royal's steep slopes. Named by Jacques Cartier in 1535 (see p32), the protected district of Parc du Mont-Royal covers more than 343 acres of forested mountain, providing abundant green spaces, shrubs and flowers, as well as habitats for hundreds of species of birds and other wildlife. Designed in 1876 by Frederick Law Olmsted, Mont-Royal continues to inspire locals as an arboreal delight in the center of their metropolis – activity options, depending on the time of year, include skating, cycling, paddle-boating, tobogganing and snowshoeing. To the northwest of the park is the impressive Oratoire St-Joseph.*

*Centre de la Montagne*

If visiting Montréal in winter you can still enjoy a version of the Tam-Tam Festival, as well as a drink, at the nearby El Zaz Bar *(see p78).*

Parking fees are high in Parc du Mont-Royal. Park your car inside the grounds of one of the cemeteries and walk to the summit lookout.

• Map C2
• (514) 843 8240
• www.lemontroyal. qc.ca
• Dis. access
• Free
• Oratoire St-Joseph: 3800 chemin Queen-Mary; (514) 733 8211; Mass: 7am, 8:30am, 10am, 11:30am, 12:15pm, 4:30pm & 7:30pm Mon–Fri; 4:30pm & 8pm Sat; 7am, 8am, 9:30am, 11am, 12:30pm, 4:30pm & 8pm Sun; Dis. access; Free; www.saint-joseph.org

## Top 10 Sights

1. La Croix
2. Trail Systems
3. Lookouts
4. Cemeteries
5. Lac aux Castors
6. Police Stables
7. Maison Smith
8. Centre de la Montagne
9. Tam-Tam Festival
10. Oratoire St-Joseph

### La Croix
Standing 31 m (100 ft) high *(right)*, the original steel cross was erected by Paul de Chomede, Sieur de Maisonneuve on this site in 1643.

### Trail Systems
The park has a network of forested corridors, popular with cyclists and runners in summer and cross-country skiers in winter.

### Lookouts
Belvedere Kondiaronk *(below)* is the lookout of the Chalet du Mont-Royal. The Camilien Houde lookout faces east over the river. Locals sometimes refer to it as "Lovers' Lookout."

### Cemeteries
Cimetière Notre-Dame-des-Neiges (Catholic) and Cimetière Mont-Royal (non-Catholic) are the two main resting places of the city. Far from sombre, they are adorned with lovely statues, sculptures and luxuriant plantings.

**Lac aux Castors**
The heart of Parc du Mont-Royal is Lac aux Castors. People gather during fair weather to paddle boats *(above)* or to ice skate in winter.

**Map of Parc du Mont-Royal**

**Police Stables**
Visits to the Police Cavalry Stables are possible, and it is common to see officers on horseback cantering through the park.

**Maison Smith**
Built for Boston merchant Hosea B. Smith in 1858, Maison Smith *(below)* is now home to the Centre de la Montagne exhibitions.

**Oratoire St-Joseph**
The dome atop this shrine is an overwhelming sight to the west of the park. Pilgrims flock to the oratory *(above)*, inspired by tales of miracle cures *(see pp10–11)*.

**Centre de la Montagne**
This is the base of a citizen group focusing on the preservation of and education about both the historic and natural legacy of the park.

**Tam-Tam Festival**
Sundays in the park during the summer belong to the exuberant Tam-Tam Festival *(left)*. For more than 30 years drummers, musicians, dancers and artisans have met at the Monument Sir George-Étienne Cartier to party.

**Frederick Law Olmsted**
A champion of the City Beautiful movement of landscape architects, Frederick Law Olmsted was born in Hartford, Connecticut in 1822. Best known for his visionary designs of Central Park in New York City, Olmsted's aim was to reject the formal plantations that had previously been in vogue and to complement the natural landscape with his pastoral designs and designated areas for recreation.

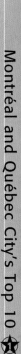

*A new heritage status protects the Parc du Mont-Royal from commercial development.*

Left **Oratoire St-Joseph façade** Right **300 steps**

# Features of Oratoire St-Joseph

### 1 Brother André
Alfred Bessette, born in 1845, joined the Congregation of the Holy Cross in 1870. Here, as a humble cleric, he assumed the name of Brother André and began working extraordinary curative powers on the sick. He attributed his skills to St Joseph's intervention and petitioned for donations to build the Oratoire.

### 2 Neo-Classical Architecture
Inspired by the temples of Corinth, architects Dalbé Viau and Alphonse Venne designed the exterior of St Joseph's, but the completion of the project was a collaboration of Lucien Parent, monk Dom Paul Bellot and architect Gérard Notebaert.

### 3 Musée de St-Joseph
An extensive religious art collection heads the permanent features on display in the

**Stained-glass window, Crypt Church**

Museum of St Joseph. A fascinating wax figure exhibition depicts the life of the Holy Family in scenarios created by Canadian artist Joseph Guardo.

### 4 Crypt Church
Created in 1917 at the foot of the basilica, the crypt church has a main altar of Carrara marble. Jean-Charles Charest, a Montréal artist, has renovated the sanctuary with a new tabernacle, lectern, colonnade, and oak chairs. Don't miss the stunning stained-glass windows.

### 5 300 Stairs
It is common to see a pilgrim struggling up the 300 steps to the basilica on his knees. Since many climb each year, plans to refurbish the stairs are in place, to the tune of $8 million.

### 6 Pilgrims' Pavilion
A convenient overnight hostel adjacent to the parking area contains a souvenir shop and cafeteria. A resident organization also helps arrange personalized religious journeys for the faithful.

### 7 Votive Chapel
Canes, crutches and other medical aids left behind by cured pilgrims line the walls in this small but inspirational chapel. Visitors can light a devotional candle, then walk past a statue of St Joseph to the room of Brother André's tomb.

*The best way to explore the Oratoire is to take one of the organized tours that begin at the visitors' pavilion.*

### Brother André's Tomb

**8** Brother André died on January 6, 1937, at the age of 91. A beautiful fresco, created by Henri Charlier, decorates his tomb wall. Also here is a register of millions of pilgrim signatures seeking canonization for the venerable Brother.

### Altar and Stations of the Cross

**9** The magnificent altar, crucifix and wooden statues of the 12 Apostles are creations of the French artist Henri Charlier. Roger Villiers sculpted the Way of the Cross between 1957–9; the stunning interior mosaic was added to the altar in 1960.

Altar and Crucifix

### Les Petits Chanteurs du Mont-Royal

**10** Begun in 1956 by the then head of the church Father Brault, the oratory's choir is made up of 210 boys aged between 8 and 17. Their silky vocals embellish more than 70 religious festivities each year, both at the oratory, around the country, and abroad. The boys receive their schooling here when they are not performing.

## The History of the Oratoire St-Joseph

*The saga of Montréal's mammoth Oratoire St-Joseph began with the construction of a tiny chapel in 1904 by Brother André and friends. However the final structural elements only came together in 1967 – 30 years after Brother André's death. More than 150 m (500 ft) above street level, it is a staggering 60 m (195 ft) from the floor to the peak of the dome – the second largest in the world after St-Peter's in Rome. Reminiscent of Italian Renaissance architecture, the basilica features Corinthian columns, stained-glass masterpieces, and one of the largest carillons in North America (56 bells). More than two million visitors pack the monument each year, with crutches and wheelchairs left behind as evidence of the continuing cures taking place here. Brother André's followers are convinced of his powers and are attempting to secure his canonization. In accordance with the Catholic church, two posthumous miracles are needed to earn a sainthood. In 1982, with the cure of a cancer victim, Pope John Paul II recognized the first miracle; André's followers eagerly await a second.*

Brother André

*Visit early in the morning or late afternoon to avoid the crowds.*

# 🔟 Basilique Notre-Dame

*The most magnificent landmark of Vieux-Montréal is this mammoth Gothic Revival undertaking designed by Irish architect James O'Donnell and built between 1824–9. This thriving Catholic church has a stunning medieval-style interior that features walnut-wood carvings, exquisite stained-glass windows, 24-carat gold stars in a vaulted blue ceiling, as well as one of the largest Casavant organs in North America. Don't miss the fine art paintings in the nave and the impressive Chapelle du Sacré-Coeur hidden behind the altar.*

🍴 **Claude Postel Chocolatier (75 Notre-Dame Ouest)** serves incredible sandwiches, coffee and desserts.

⭐ Breathtaking sound and light *(son et lumière)* shows are worth attending during April, May and June.

• 110 rue Notre-Dame Ouest, Place d'Armes
• Map K3
• (514) 842 2925
• Open 8:15am–4:30pm Mon–Fri, 8:15am–4pm Sat, 12:30–4pm Sun
• Adm $5
• www.basilique nddm.org

## Top 10 Features

1. Gothic Revival Architecture
2. Stained-Glass Windows
3. Le Gros Bourdon
4. Casavant Organ
5. The Altar
6. The Pulpit
7. Chapelle du Sacré-Coeur
8. Daudelin Sculpting
9. Famous Weddings
10. Séminaire St-Sulpice

### Gothic Revival Architecture
Rectangular in shape, contrary to the norms of the day, Notre-Dame features arcades with cross-ribbed vaulting.

### Stained-Glass Windows
In 1929 Olivier Maurault, a priest and author, conceived the present-day windows, which depict both early religious events as well as scenes from the everyday lives of people of Vieux-Montréal.

### Le Gros Bourdon
It is possible to hear the amazing chimes of Le Gros Bourdon, the largest bell in North America, some 30 km (18 miles) outside Montréal.

### Casavant Organ
Joseph Casavant was a Québécois blacksmith and the first significant builder of pipe organs in Canada. He built the famous Notre-Dame organ *(left)* for the basilica in 1891.

### 6 The Pulpit

Architect Victor Bourgeau's first known work is the 1844 spiral staircase pulpit *(left)*, which some say resembles the tiers of a wedding cake. Set in the middle of the church, it allows the congregation to hear sermons without amplification.

### 7 Chapelle du Sacré-Coeur

Opened in 1891, this gem *(above)* hides behind the main altar. Countless marriage ceremonies take place here, inspiring the moniker, "The Wedding Chapel."

### 8 Daudelin Sculpting

Sculptor Charles Daudelin's bronze *reredos (below)*, which hangs behind the Chapelle du Sacré-Coeur, is among his most dramatic works.

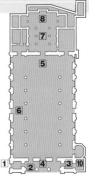

**Plan of Basilique Notre-Dame**

### 10 Séminaire St-Sulpice

Built in 1685 by the Sulpician order, this structure beside the basilica *(below)* is the oldest building in Montréal *(see p55)*.

### James O'Donnell

Irish architect James O'Donnell was contracted to draw plans and oversee the construction of Basilique Notre-Dame in 1823. A Protestant by birth, O'Donnell's pride in the basilica caused him to convert to Catholicism, allowing him burial inside "his" church. Synthesizing many divergent design elements from contributing architects, he introduced the Gothic Revival style into Canadian architecture.

### 5 The Altar

In 1880 local artists Henri Bouriché and Victor Bourgeau created complementary wood sculptings backed by azure for this spectacular altarpiece *(above)*.

### 9 Famous Weddings

Many famous couples have tied the knot in Notre-Dame but the most mentioned celebrity wedding is that of recording star Céline Dion in 1994 *(see p39)*.

*Architect James O'Donnell is buried at the foot of the first column on the side of the churchwarden's pew.*

Montréal and Québec City's Top 10

13

# Parc Olympique

*One of Montréal's most remarkable attractions, Parc Olympique is also one of its most controversial. Built for the 1976 Olympic Games, it remained unfinished until the 1980s, despite a cost of $1.4 billion, and the retractable roof over the stadium has never fully worked. Nevertheless, visitors can easily spend a full day or two entertained by the varied exhibitions, sights and activities available within this immense quadrilateral. Ride the funicular to the top of the Tour Montréal for the most enthralling view of the region.*

Stade Olympique and Tour Montréal

🍽 The best place to eat, for both price and atmosphere, is Moe's Deli on rue Sherbrooke *(see p78)*.

🎯 "Montréal in Motion" is a free photography exhibition capturing 100 years of the city's history, located in the Observatory on top of the Tour Montréal.

• 4141 rue Pierre-de-Coubertin
• Métro Pie-IX
• (514) 252 4737
• www.rio.gouv.qc.ca
• Adm to specific attractions
• Jardin Botanique; 4101 rue Sherbrooke Est; (514) 872 1400; Open mid-May–early Sep: 9am–6pm daily, early Sep–end Oct: 9am–9pm daily; Nov–mid-May: 9am–5pm daily; Closed Mon in Jan–May, Nov, & Dec Dis. access; Adm; www2.ville.montreal. qc.ca/jardin

## Top 10 Sights

1. Stade Olympique
2. Aréna Maurice-Richard
3. Biodome
4. Insectarium
5. Jardin Botanique
6. Tour Montréal
7. Marché Maisonneuve
8. Musée Château Dufresne
9. Centre Sportif
10. Village Olympique Condos

### Stade Olympique
Designed by the French architect Roger Taillibert and constructed by local engineers for the 1976 Olympics, the stadium *(right)* seats 65,000 people, has a cable-suspended roof and is covered in a membrane of space-age Kevlar material. Today it is used to stage events such as rock concerts.

### Aréna Maurice-Richard
Named after the Montréal Canadiens hockey legend Maurice "Rocket" Richard, the indoor rink *(above)* continues to promote the sport. The museum "Univers Maurice-Richard" features the scoring ace's memorabilia.

### Biodome
The Biodome houses dazzling ecological attractions, with indigenous plants and animals of the Tropical Forest, Polar World *(below)* and Laurentian Forest.

### Insectarium
Quebecer Georges Brossard, known as "the Bug Man," roams the world collecting exotic insects then displays them in this riveting showcase (above).

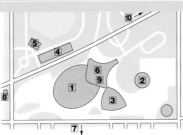

**Map of Parc Olympique**

### Jardin Botanique
Founded in 1931 and covering nearly 200 acres, the lush gardens were created by gifted horticulturist Henry Teuscher (see pp16–17).

### Tour Montréal
For the best view of Montréal ride the extraordinary, 2-minute, 76-seat funicular in the Tour Montréal (above). An observatory sits atop the world's highest leaning tower, almost 175 m (585 ft) from ground to summit.

### Marché Maisonneuve
More than just a taste of fresh market fare, the Marché Maisonneuve also provides a gathering point. Attracting clientele from all over the city and the province, the market is a great spot for people-watching.

### Musée Château Dufresne
The Gothic-inspired private residence (left), was originally designed and constructed by Parisian architect Jules Rénard for Oscar and Marius Dufresne from 1915 to 1918. It now welcomes a variety of decorative exhibitions.

### Centre Sportif
This sports complex houses five swimming pools with continuously recirculating water (below). Other resources include badminton courts, a scuba diving club, volleyball, and more.

### Village Olympique Condos
An elegant, multi-tiered structure built to house athletes for the 1976 games is now a desirable set of condominiums.

### Mayor Jean Drapeau
Many agree that the enthusiasm of Jean Drapeau, the mayor of Montréal from 1954–7 and again from 1960–86 (see p33), put Montréal on the international map. A lawyer by trade, he was passionate about his city, and while in office oversaw the building of the Métro subway system and the city's cultural venue Place des Arts, brought the World's Fair to town in 1967 and led the successful bid for the 1976 Olympic Games.

Left & Right **Chinese Gardens**

# 10 Jardin Botanique Features

### Greenhouses
A series of greenhouses in the gardens, just past the entrance, provide enough humidity for various botanical environments to thrive, including a rainforest canopy, tropical medicinal plants, and beautiful, brightly colored orchids.

### Chinese Gardens
A classic example of a Ming Dynasty garden, complete with its own Lac du Rêve *(Lake of Dreams, see below)*. This garden covers over 6 acres and is lovingly nurtured by specialist teams from both Montréal and Shanghai. These are the largest Chinese gardens outside China.

### Lac du Rêve
A lush domain in the center of the Chinese Gardens, where visitors can watch resident geese and ducks, find a comfortable area to relax, or just wander through the landscaped lake area surrounded by rock gardens, bridges and areas for reflection.

### First Nations Garden
The First Nations (native Canadians) celebrate their magical relationship with the plant kingdom within these 6 acres of gardens filled with interactive terminals, shows and special events. The area is divided up into five different zones: hardwood and softwood forests, an exploration of Nordic life, an interpretation pavilion, and a gathering area.

### Sukiya Japanese Tea Pavilion
Honoring the traditional Japanese home, architect Hisato Hiraoka has gathered together the artistic ideals of Japanese society within this graceful structure. There is also an art gallery, Zen and bonsai gardens, an exhibition room and a gift shop.

### Wu Yee-Sun Bonsai Collection
At any time of year, in any kind of weather, the captivating Wu Yee-Sun Collection of miniature bonsai trees is on permanent exhibit inside their greenhouse. This is one of the most impressive and largest collections of its kind in the world.

### Treehouse
This remarkable interpretation center and interactive exhibition is laid out in four parts: Trees in our History, Anatomy and Growth, Trees and the

**Lac du Rêve**

*For opening times to the gardens* **See p14**

Forest, and The Many Uses of Trees. The Treehouse exhibit is located in the northeast sector of the gardens.

### 8 Ballade
Since the gardens spread over many acres, take advantage of the popular Ballade minibus circulating continuously throughout the day along the paved pathways. Clearly marked areas within the gardens indicate where buses make regular stops.

**Bonsai tree**

### 9 Libraries
Two fascinating libraries are situated within the gardens. The public library boasts an extensive children's section and there is an academic library that is home to numerous scientific books, journals and papers, including studies of botany.

### 10 Children's Highlights
Exciting and informative permanent features in the garden are part of the on-going effort to educate Montréal children and bring them closer to nature. Exhibitions that are exclusively for kids include the Youth Garden, Butterflies Go Free, Noah's Ark, the Hallowe'en Mask Competition and the Chlorophyll Room. Each season boasts an additional theme.

**Top 10 Flora in the Jardin Botanique**

1. Aroids
2. Begonias
3. Bonsai & penjing
4. Ferns
5. Bromeliads
6. Cacti & succulents
7. Cyads
8. Orchids
9. Lilacs & lotus
10. Gesneriads

## History of the Jardin Botanique

*In 1931, Montréal's then-mayor, Camillien Houde, conceived of a master plan to put the unemployed to work by building the city's first botanical gardens. He hired architect Lucien Keroack to design the main building, and work began in the midst of a deep economic depression. Owing much to the Christian Brothers religious sect and particularly to Brother Marie-Victorin for his visionary concept, the team invited American landscape architect and botanist Henry Teuscher to establish the permanent collections and design the site. By 1938 the greenhouses were built and Montréal has presented this rich horticultural domain ever since.*

**Opening the Gardens**
When it opened in 1938 the Jardin Botanique was second only to London's Kew Gardens in size. With a team of expert gardeners it continues to thrive, despite the city's harsh winters.

*In the fall, the Magic of Lanterns festival displays 600 Chinese lanterns in the gardens to celebrate the harvest.*

17

# 10 Musée Pointe-à-Callière

*Ascending like a sentinel from the confluence of the St Pierre and St Lawrence rivers, this National Historic Site honors the founding of the city at Place Royale. Within this landmark of stone and brushed steel are three sections: a chic building constructed on top of the ruins of older structures; the archeological crypt; and the renovated Customs House. A self-guided tour system allows each visitor to explore at their own pace, but guides are employed throughout the site to answer questions. These escorts are accomplished storytellers, bringing the history of the city to life.*

*Old Customs House*

One of the best views in all of Vieux-Montréal is available from Café L'Arrivage on the top level of the museum. It serves good but expensive bistro cuisine.

- 350 Place Royale at rue de la Commune
- Map K3
- (514) 872 9150
- www.pacmuseum.qc.ca
- Open 10am–5pm Tue–Fri, 11am–5pm Sat–Sun
- Dis. access
- Adm $13 adults; $9 senior citizens; $7.50 students; $5 children; under 6s free

### Top 10 Exhibits

1. Éperon Building
2. Tales of a City
3. First Catholic Cemetery in North America
4. Where Montréal Was Born
5. Underground Vaulted Conduit
6. Models At Your Feet
7. A Customs House and its Architect
8. Youville Pumping Station Interpretation Center
9. Market Day, 1750
10. Montréal Love Stories

### Éperon Building
Architect Dan S. Hanganu designed this edifice *(right)* to create a building that is an exhibition in itself. The front door marks the spot of the first shelter in Ville-Marie (1642).

### Tales of a City
One of the most inspired introductions to any museum, this 18-minute voyage through the discovery of Montréal enchants visitors and sets the stage for a memorable visit.

### First Catholic Cemetery in North America
Residents of the original fortification created a cemetery under Place Royale. When the museum excavated the site, the discovery resulted in this exhibit *(right)*.

### Where Montréal Was Born
This exhibition represents more than 600 years of local history, from Amerindian times to the present day.

*Share your travel recommendations on traveldk.com*

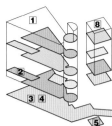

**Plan of Musée Pointe-à-Callière**

**Key**

| | Basement |
| | Ground Floor |
| | First Floor |
| | Second Floor |
| | Third Floor |
| | Fourth Floor |

### 6 Models At Your Feet

Virtual technology bridges past with present here. Meet historic figures, hear archeological explanations and view five centuries of artifacts under glass beneath your feet.

### 9 Market Day, 1750

This interactive virtual fresco is set in the archaelogical remains of the main gate that led to the marketplace in 1750. Visitors can bring to life various figures, who emerge from the stores and play out scenes from their lives.

### 7 A Customs House and its Architect

Montréal's old Customs House, built between 1836 and 1837, is a Neo-Classical building designed by John Ostell, a local architect. It has been carefully renovated to its original state by the museum.

### 10 Montréal Love Stories

This series of intimate portraits of the city *(above)* draws on photographs, videos, and first-hand accounts of Montréalers.

### 5 Underground Vaulted Conduit

Montréal's earliest plumbing and sewer system, dating from the 18th century, can be seen in this network of conduits, beneath a cobblestoned walkway *(right)*. Another excavation revealed the tiny St Pierre River, now permanently below ground.

### 8 Youville Pumping Station Interpretation Center

Across from the museum an old pumping station has exhibits on science and technology.

### History of the Museum

In 1642 Paul de Chomedey, Sieur de Maisonneuve, founded the settlement of Ville-Marie, now Montréal, on this site. More than 350 years later, a series of excavations unearthed the way of life for these newcomers to Nouvelle-France and Musée Pointe-à-Callière opened with over one million artifacts. A permanent archeological dig is now in place in the area.

# 🔟 Musée des Beaux-Arts de Montréal

*One of the most impressive museums in North America dominates both sides of stately rue Sherbrooke Ouest. It began life in 1860, when a group of collectors set up the Art Association of Montréal to present exhibitions, establish an art school, assemble a permanent collection of paintings and develop an art library. The members eventually raised finances to construct their own building, now the Michal & Renata Hornstein Pavilion, to house Old Masters and contemporary works. In 1991 the museum expanded into the modern Jean-Noël Desmarais Pavilion (illustrated here), on the south side of the street.*

Jean-Noël Desmarais
Pavilion façade

🍽 The on-site **Café des Beaux-Arts serves delicious but expensive French bistro cuisine** *(see p72),* **but there is an inexpensive cafeteria in the same area of the Jean-Noël Desmarais Pavilion.**

• 1379–80 rue
Sherbrooke Ouest
• Map C3
• (514) 285 2000
• www.mmfa.qc.ca
• Open 11am–5pm Tue,
11am–9pm Wed–Fri,
10am–5pm Sat & Sun
• Dis. access
• Free

## Top 10 Paintings

1. Portrait of a Young Woman
2. Apelles Painting the Portrait of Campaspe
3. Octobre
4. Judith with the Head of Holopherne, Didon
5. The Tribute Money
6. Portrait of the Lawyer Hugo Simons
7. Venice, Looking out over the Lagoon
8. The Wheel
9. The Black Star
10. Mauve Twilight

### Octobre

An example of James Tissot's control and mastery of space, this 1877 allegorical work is of model Kathleen Irene Newton. It was painted in London after the demise of the Commune of Paris in 1871.

### Portrait of a Young Woman

A combined use of light, color, texture and setting bring a feeling of intimacy to this 1665 Rembrandt work *(above).*

### Apelles Painting the Portrait of Campaspe

Italian artist Tiepolo uses the unusual technique of a painting-within-a-painting in this 1726 work. Notice the artwork hanging on the wall of the studio, which is one of Tiepolo's own, entitled *The Bronze Serpent.*

### The Wheel
Montréal's best-known contemporary painter, Jean-Paul Riopelle, lets his spatula work its magic on this canvas (1954–5), creating a mosaic of elements, colors and tones (left). Riopelle's signature is his chaotic style and some affinity to the brushwork of Cézanne.

### The Black Star
Paul-Émile Borduas began as a church decorator before attending the École des Beaux-Arts in Montréal and finishing his studies in France. This 1957 painting won a posthumous Guggenheim award in 1960 as the best Canadian painting in a New York gallery, but the work has now returned to the artist's home town.

### The Tribute Money
Philippe de Champaigne's 1655 work portrays the Biblical tale of the Pharisees in this dramatic religious painting. The figure on the right is said to be a self-portrait and borrows stylistically from Raphael and Valentin.

### Mauve Twilight
Painted in 1921, this work, in the Michal & Renata Hornstein Pavilion, provides an evocative impression of winter by one of Québec's most loved artists, Ozias Leduc. His ability to capture the light of dusk here confirms his legacy for perfectly representing the provincial landscape.

### Portrait of the Lawyer Hugo Simons
Otto Dix's artistic freedom is evident in this 1929 portrait of lawyer Hugo Simons. Seen with a halo of copper light, it illustrates the artist's wish to portray his subjects' souls in his works.

### Venice, Looking out over the Lagoon
A great voyeur of the human landscape, Morrice is known for his departure from centuries of art tradition and for his philosophy of painting for painting's sake, seen in this work.

### Key to Floor Plan
- Level S2
- Level 3
- Level 4

### Judith with the Head of Holopherne, Didon
Created as two paintings (1500), Andrea Mantegna here displays classic Renaissance elements: absence of emotion, knowledge of anatomy and determinism of line.

### Museum Guide
There are three pavilions that make up the museum; the Michal and Renata Hornstein Pavilion (Canadian and Inuit art collection), which contains the Liliane and David M, Stewart Pavilion featuring decorative arts. The Jean-Noël Desmarais Pavilion, across the street and connected via a tunnel from Level S2, features European art. Entrance to the museum complex is possible at either address.

21

# 🔟 La Citadelle, Québec City

*Dramatically set atop Cap Diamant, this installation of 10 buildings is the largest military fortification (40 acres) in North America. Overlooking the St Lawrence River, the site was begun by the French in 1750, but much of the striking star-shaped battlement seen today was constructed by the British between 1820 and 1850, built to defend the city from possible invasion from the United States in the 19th century. The fort is an active home to the Royal 22nd Regiment of the Canadian Army and daily military spectacles are staged to entertain visitors during the summer months.*

*Dalhousie Gate*

🍴 There are no refreshment facilities inside La Citadelle, but you are welcome to bring a picnic.

⏰ The Changing of the Guard takes place daily at 10am from late June to September and lasts about 35 minutes.

- Côte de la Citadelle
- Map L6
- (418) 694 2815
- www.lacitadelle.qc.ca
- Open daily
- Dis. access
- Adm $10 adults; $9 students and senior citizens; $5.50 children; $22 families (free for children under 7 and disabled visitors)

## Top 10 Features

1. Outer Walls
2. Dalhousie Gate
3. Changing of the Guard
4. Fortifications
5. Barracks
6. Chapel
7. Redoubt
8. Governor-General's Residence
9. Firing of the Cannon
10. Museums

### Outer Walls
In 1820, under the British Lieutenant-Colonel Elias Walker Durnford, building of the outer walls of the polygon structure began *(right)*. No one could access the Great Lakes or the Atlantic Ocean without coming under the watchful eye of La Citadelle's forces.

### Dalhousie Gate
Named in honor of Castle Dalhousie in Scotland, this formal entrance provides general access to La Citadelle and is the point at which processions and parades enter the grounds.

### Changing of the Guard
One of the most entertaining military exercises involves precision marching with a musical escort. It is headed by Batisse the goat, the regiment's mascot.

### Fortifications
The fortress *(left)* contains the most important elements for a military installation: height over the enemy; 360-degree visibility; difficult access; and durability. Having all of this to its advantage, La Citadelle has never once been attacked by an enemy.

### Barracks
**5** A large part of the site is given over to housing the troops. Tanks used in past battles by the regiment are also on display *(above)*.

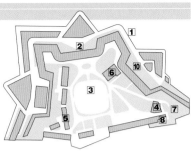

**Plan of La Citadelle**

### Firing of the Cannon
**9** The dramatic firing of the cannon takes place at the Citadelle every day at noon and at 9:30pm during the summer. It's a fine illustration of the military might the fort once displayed.

### Museums
**10** The collections unveiled in the two museums located here include everyday items used by soldiers over the centuries, a collection of rare military documents, ceremonial uniforms, antique armaments, precious art and other eclectic items.

### Chapel
**6** Since army life requires servicemen to work far from home for long periods, every effort was made to include elements of everyday life at the fortification, including a chapel *(above)*.

### Redoubt
**7** Tucked away into sections of the fieldstone walls, cannons protect their flanks without the need for backup support.

### Governor-General's Residence
**8** Since Samuel de Champlain's tenure in the 1600s the Governor-General has resided here *(below)* during the summer.

### Royal 22nd Regiment
Since 1969 the Royal 22nd Régiment's 2nd Battalion has provided the Guard for La Citadelle. This prestigious group was honored for their bravery during the Korean War (1950–53) and for numerous other peacekeeping roles since then. The splendor of Québec City's summer is heightened each day by military ceremonies such as the Changing of the Guard. The pomp of this pageant is highlighted by the scarlet uniforms and the regimental brass band.

# Musée de la Civilisation de Québec

*Few museums in the world receive the kind of rave reviews given to the MCQ. The exhibitions (two of which are permanent) cover history, culture, sports, science, and intellectual and esoteric themes in a range of interactive ways that entertain and educate visitors. Designed by the celebrated architect Moshe Safdie, creator of Ottawa's National Gallery, the MCQ incorporates the Musée de l'Amérique Française, the Maison Chevalier, the Séminaire de Québec, as well as the Place-Royale Interpretation Center, to produce this vibrant look at local life in all its facets. The main entrance is the rue Dalhousie site.*

*Musée de la Civilisation façade*

🍽 Good food at a reasonable price is found at the on-site cafeteria near the coat-check area.

✪ Do not try to see everything the MCQ offers at their three locations in one day. For a more enjoyable experience, plan to attend only those parts that you are most interested in.

• 85 rue Dalhousie, Basse-Ville, Québec City
• Map M4
• (418) 643 2158
• www.mcq.org
• Open 10am–5pm Tue–Sun; mid-June–Labor Day: 9:30am–6:30pm daily
• Adm $11 adults; $10 senior citizens; $8 students; $4 children; under 11s free (free to all every Tue in winter)

## Top 10 Exhibitions

1. The Chapel of the Séminaire de Québec
2. Encounter with First Nations
3. Musée de l'Amérique Française
4. Place-Royale, A Québec Toujours: La Marque de Champlain
5. Maison Chevalier
6. Centre d'Interprétation de Place-Royale
7. Séminaire de Québec
8. People of Québec ...Then and Now
9. Make Way for the Middle Ages
10. Joseph the Boarder

### The Chapel of the Séminaire de Québec
Information about Catholic rites and church decoration can be found here.

### Encounter with First Nations
A magnificent exhibition of First Nations' treasures *(right)*, with over 500 objects covering the history of the native Canadians.

### Musée de l'Amérique Française
The oldest museum in Canada features more than 450,000 artifacts from the earliest French communities.

### Place-Royale, A Québec Toujours: La Marque de Champlain
This exhibit opened in 2008 to mark the 400th anniversary of Samuel de Champlain's arrival here.

### Maison Chevalier
Jean-Baptiste Chevalier's 18th-century home *(left)* has been lovingly restored and includes the Living Heritage Workshop, a series of tutorials focusing on traditional French customs, music and dance since the days of early settlement.

### 6 Centre d'Interprétation de place-Royale
Daily life as it was in Nouvelle-France comes alive at Place-Royale; historic celebrations are regularly mounted on the site of the first settlement.

**Map of Museum Sites**

### 7 Séminaire de Québec
Three outstanding exhibitions in the seminary *(above)* form the largest religious collection in North America. The artifacts document the early religious education of the city.

### 9 Make Way for the Middle Ages
Based around the workings of a medieval French village, this costume workshop explores how aspects of life in the Middle Ages have influenced how we live in the modern age.

### 10 Joseph the Boarder
An enchanting interactive presentation, located in the Jérome-Demers Pavilion, recalls daily life in Le Petit Séminaire de Québec for "Joseph," a typical waif in the early days of Nouvelle-France.

### 8 People of Québec ...Then and Now
Visitors can relive 400 years of Québec's history, meeting figures from yesterday and connecting to a past that is still shaping events of today. Original and archival film clips *(right)* from the National Film Board enliven the exhibit along the way.

### Separatism
Ever since the British made an offer in 1848 to allow the French to maintain their language within an English-speaking domain, the relationship between what would become the nation of Canada and the province of Québec has been fraught with mistrust. As Canada and Québec continually reached political deadlock, separatist sentiment grew. Many Québécois feel that their province is distinct from the rest of Canada, and so would be better off as a separate nation. In 1980 and 1995, the province held referendums on whether to separate, and both times the vote was a narrow "no."

# TOP 10 Basilique Sainte-Anne-de-Beaupré

*The oldest pilgrimage site in North America began life in 1658 as a shrine to this patron saint of Québec and was established as a basilica in 1887. The present church, started in 1923 but only completed in 1963, has a striking interior with sumptuous decoration, including impressive window archways. Hundreds of crutches, canes and medical aids can be seen stacked in pyramids beside the medieval-style entrance, testimony to pilgrim prayer and the healing powers associated with Sainte Anne de Beaupré. Stunning religious statues frame the entrance and line the luxurious gardens, including a Way of the Cross.*

Stained-glass window

🍽 Restaurant L'ainé is located two minutes from the basilica and serves delicious home-cooked meals at affordable prices.

🌀 Call ahead for information regarding any special celebrations or festivities, since the crowds can be an impediment to enjoying the site.

• 10018 ave Royale, Sainte-Anne-de-Beaupré
• Map P3
• (418) 827 3781
• www.ssadb.qc.ca
• Open daily
• Free
• Musée de Sainte-Anne: Open May–Oct: daily; Adm

## Top 10 Features

1. Medieval Architecture
2. Stained-Glass Windows
3. Candlelight Processions
4. Way of the Cross Bronzes
5. Memorial Chapel
6. St Augustin
7. Scala Santa
8. Musée de Sainte-Anne
9. Cyclorama de Jérusalem
10. Atelier Paré

### 1 Medieval Architecture

A five-nave towered church *(right & below)* blends imposing Gothic architecture with Romanesque details previously unseen in Québec Province.

### 2 Stained-Glass Windows

The dazzling 240 stained-glass windows depict moments in the life of Ste Anne. The centerpiece is a huge oval window flooding light into the nave.

### 3 Candlelight Processions

It is common to witness evening candlelight processions honoring saints and religious holidays; those on July 25 and 26 celebrate Ste Anne.

### Way of the Cross Bronzes

Life-size bronze statues *(above)* line the hillside trail beside the basilica. Honouring saints and Apostles, these artworks infuse a Renaissance feeling to the grounds.

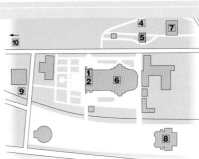

**Plan of Basilique Ste-Anne-de-Beaupré**

### St Augustin

Thomas Baillairgé continued his family's legacy as a religious decorator by carving pieces for the basilica, including a statue of St Augustin.

### Scala Santa

A wonderful little chapel constructed in 1891 *(above)* includes a remarkable stairway venerating the one Jesus ascended to face condemnation by Pontius Pilate.

### Musée de Sainte-Anne

A separate building next to the main shrine features two floors of religious exhibitions focusing on Ste Anne and the 300 years of pilgrimage to this holy site.

### Cyclorama de Jérusalem

The world's largest panoramic painting *(above)* was created in Munich between 1878–82. It was shipped in sections in 1895 and still transfixes visitors with its overview of Jerusalem.

### Atelier Paré

This woodcarver's workshop is worth a visit to see the artisan at work creating pieces for the basilica.

### Sainte Anne de Beaupré

Records of Ste Anne, mother of the Virgin Mary, begin in the 2nd century and a cult of Ste Anne is referred to as early as the 5th century. She is the patroness of housewives, cabinet-makers, miners and the Province of Québec. She features frequently in works of art, including some by Leonardo da Vinci. Her name derives from the Hebrew *Hannah*, meaning "grace."

**Memorial Chapel**

This votive chapel *(right)*, built in 1878 to commemorate the original church on this site, contains religious memorabilia, rare documents and artifacts.

Atelier Paré is two minutes from the shrine on avenue Royale and provides an opportunity to purchase unusual souvenirs.

# 🔟 Ile d'Orléans

*A haven of greenery and tranquility, Ile d'Orléans was one of the first European settlements in the New World and is referred to as the cradle of French civilization in North America. Ever since Jacques Cartier arrived here in 1535, the six parishes along this 30-km (18-mile) island have maintained many of the French traditions of the first settlers, and over 600 heritage buildings present a preserved architectural gem. The fertile soil means that the island's produce has become known as the area's open-air market.*

Auberge la Goeliche sign

🍴 Auberge Restaurant Le Canard Huppé in the village of St-Laurent *(2198 chemin Royal • 1-800-838-2292)* will spoil you with fine cuisine. They also have B&B rooms if you want to stay overnight. There are also many other B&B accommodations across the island.

🚲 The tranquility of this island makes it a perfect spot to rent a bicycle, follow the walking guide from the Interpretation Center or enjoy a picnic at one of the idyllic spots beside the river.

• Dufferin-Montmorency highway 440
• Map P3
• Bureau d'information touristique: 490 côte du Pont, St-Pierre-de-l'Ile-d'Orléans; (418) 828 9411; www. iledorleans.com

## Top 10 Sights

1. Ile de Bacchus
2. Montmorency Falls
3. Interpretation Center
4. Auberge la Goeliche
5. Chocolaterie de l'Ile d'Orléans
6. Le Vignoble Ste-Pétronille
7. Horatio Walker Studio
8. Domain Steinbach
9. La Forge-à-Pique-Assaut
10. Manoir Mauvide-Genest

### Ile de Bacchus
When Jacques Cartier found vines here he named it Ile de Bacchus after the Greek god of wine, then changed the name to honor the Duke of Orléans.

### Montmorency Falls
Higher than Niagara Falls, Montmorency Falls *(right)* are a dramatic sight before you cross the bridge onto the island *(see p100)*.

### Interpretation Center
The Centre d'Interprétation rents out their $10 tape or CD guide which you can play in your car stereo as you tour the island for a background history of the various parishes.

### Auberge la Goeliche
In the lovely community of Ste-Pétronille the Auberge la Goeliche offers guests old-world hospitality, food and ambiance.

### Chocolaterie de l'Ile d'Orléans
Ste-Pétronille is home to the most wonderful chocolate-maker in the province *(left)*, which also sells delicious homemade ice cream, jellies and other edible goodies. It also houses an interesting interpretation center that explains the process of creating chocolate.

**Map of Île d'Orléans**

### 6 Le Vignoble Ste-Pétronille
With an incredible view across the St Lawrence River to Montmorency Falls, this 50-acre vineyard is an excellent example of a quality, cold-weather grape vintner creating red, white and rosé wines (above), popular in the restaurants of Québec City.

### 8 Domain Steinbach
Domain Steinbach (below), located in St-Pierre, welcomes visitors for organic wine and cider tastings, and also makes vinegars and mustards.

### 10 Manoir Mauvide-Genest
This 1734 manor (above) is one of the oldest buildings in the province and a fine example of rural architecture from the 18th century. There's an on-site museum and a restaurant.

### 9 La Forge-à-Pique-Assaut
The forge (below) offers a fascinating opportunity to look inside a black-smith's workshop. Artisan Guy Bel labors here, admirably maintaining traditional metalworking techniques.

### 7 Horatio Walker Studio
The Canadian landscape artist Horatio Walker was a resident of the island, and his studio is preserved in Ste-Pétronille on the street renamed in his honor. His legacy continues in the work of other island painters such as Horace Champagne.

### Félix Leclerc
No mention of Île d'Orléans would be complete without reference to the spirit of the province at large, as it was embodied in the artistry of Félix Leclerc (1914–88). The legacy of this prolific singer, song-writer, poet and play-wright (see p38), and his ability to perfectly express the Québecois sensibility is honored at L'Espace Félix-Leclerc (682, chemin Royal, St-Pierre • Open daily) where there is a permanent exhibition about his work, as well as a coffee house with live entertainment and a gift shop.

# 🔟 Les Laurentides

*Les Laurentides (the Laurentians) are part of a shield of forested peaks enclosed by the Ottawa, St Lawrence and Saguenay rivers, and are best known for their magnificent ski slopes, which roll into sight one hour north of Montréal. First Nations relics indicate Amerindian settlements here over 4,000 years ago, and since the 19th century the region has been a rich agricultural zone and famous for hunting, trapping and fishing in its 6,000 lakes and ponds. Visitors can enjoy the historic Francophone villages, cycle and hike on numerous trails in summer, or sample the luxury of modern ski resorts in winter.*

*Skier, Ste-Adèle*

🍽 **L'Eureye is a Belgian restaurant in Ste-Adèle, one minute east off the Laurentian Autoroute No. 15 and worth the side-trip *(see p87).*

🌿 **Reasonably priced and comfortable log cabins are available on a first-come-first-served basis inside the Parc National de Mont-Tremblant (1-877 688 2289).**

• Map N5
• Maison de Tourisme de Laurentides: Port du Nord, Exit 51, Highway 15; (450) 224 7007; postal address: 14142 rue de la Chapelle, Mirabel; (450) 436 8532
• www.laurentides.com

## Top 10 Sights

1. St-Sauveur-des-Monts
2. Mont-Rolland
3. Ste-Adèle
4. Ville d'Estérel
5. Val-Morin
6. Val-David
7. Ste-Agathe-des-Monts
8. St-Jovite
9. Mont Tremblant
10. Parc National du Mont-Tremblant

### 1 St-Sauveur-des-Monts
Downhill skiing is the draw here in winter, but in summer the artisans' shops *(above)*, restaurants and galleries tempt visitors to town.

### 2 Mont-Rolland
The historic homes in this laid-back village were built to house workers of the Rolland Mill, once the main employer of this forested domain.

### 3 Ste-Adèle
Spectacular outdoor recreation within easy reach of Montréal attracted the first tourist train to Ste-Adèle in 1891, and the town continues to welcome ski enthusiasts today.

### 4 Ville d'Estérel
This lush, rolling area *(left)* includes Ste-Marguerite-du-Lac-Masson, the village where renowned artist Jean-Paul Riopelle painted for many years. The area was originally developed by a Belgian aristocrat in the 1930s.

### Val-Morin
Along the P'tit Train du Nord cycle path *(above)*, this tiny Francophone village beguiles visitors as the trail meanders around Lac Raymond. Skiers can enjoy slopes at Belle Neige.

**Map of les Laurentides**

### Mont Tremblant
This is the highest peak in les Laurentides at over 900 m (2,950 ft) and one of the most popular ski resorts in North America. Spas, shops, excellent dining and live entertainment all add to the appeal *(left)*.

### Parc National du Mont-Tremblant
The largest of an awe-inspiring inventory of provincial parks, it provides a safe haven for black bears, white-tailed deer, moose, wolves, and raccoons, and over 200 species of birds. Outdoor activities include hiking, canoeing, fishing, and cross-country skiing.

### Val-David
An enthralling town peppered with art galleries, music and poetry festivals, and mountain-biking contests.

### Ste-Agathe-des-Monts
With its fishing, swimming and skiing, this became the first resort in les Laurentides over 100 years ago *(below)*.

### St-Jovite
The gateway to the Mont-Tremblant commercial district, the village of St-Jovite *(above)* offers visitors boutiques and traditional Québecois restaurants. Visit the palatial Monastère des Apôtres de l'Amour Infini just east of town.

### "Jackrabbit" Johannsen
Born in Norway in 1875, Herman "Jackrabbit" Johannsen settled in the Montréal area with his wife and children in 1928. First Nations residents apparently gave him his nickname after watching him moving mysteriously and swiftly across the snow. This remarkable man, who lived an active outdoor life until the age of 111, put the Laurentian Mountains on the global ski map and brought cross-country skiing to Canada.

Left **First Nations settlement** Right **Jacques Cartier**

# 🔟 Moments in History

### 1 First Nations
Iroquoian and nomadic Algonquian peoples had lived in Québec for thousands of years when the first Europeans arrived. "Kebec" is an Algonquian word meaning "place where the river narrows."

### 2 Jacques Cartier
French explorer Cartier followed Basque fishing routes up the St Lawrence River, claiming "discovery" of Canada for King François I of France in 1534. He continued up the river in 1535 to land at the village of Hochelaga, where he named its mountain Mont Royal (see pp8–9).

### 3 Samuel de Champlain
French settlement began in 1608 when Samuel de Champlain (1567–1635) arrived in the region. The position of Québec City, protected atop Cap Diamant, became the driving force of the settlement, together with newly found riches of the fur trade.

**Samuel de Champlain**

### 4 British Takeover
The struggle between the French and British in Europe continued in the New World. In 1759, after a summer-long standoff, British General James Wolfe won claim to the province during the 30-minute siege of Québec City on the Plains of Abraham. However, in 1774 the French were granted language and religion rights (see p25).

### 5 The Creation of Canada
After the Constitutional Act (1791) separated the colony into Upper Canada (southern Ontario) and Lower Canada (southern Québec), British Lord Durham was sent to solve the on-going problems between the English and French halves. He declared the Union Act of 1841, which fused the two sides under a single English-speaking parliament and effectively marginalized the French. By 1848, the English were forced to accept the use of French to avoid a backlash. On July 1, 1867, Québec and Ontario joined with Nova Scotia and New Brunswick to form the Dominion of Canada.

### 6 The Dark Years
Well into the 20th century the Roman Catholic church held considerable political sway in Québec. Maurice Duplessis' right-wing Union Nationale (1936–39 & 1944–59) used the church's moral influence to gain votes and accepted $100-million-worth of graft.

### The Quiet Revolution

The collusion of church and state led to widespread resentment among Québécois. With the death of Duplessis, liberal sentiment grew and a lively intellectual scene developed. In 1960, the Liberal Party was elected, leading to province-wide social reforms and economic development.

### The October Crisis

Due to continuing political deadlock with Canada, support for the separatist movement among Québécois was growing. But disaster struck in October 1970 when the radical separatist Front de Libération du Québec (FLQ) kidnapped two high-ranking politicians, murdering one of them.

René Lévesque

### Parti Québécois

René Lévesque's separatist Parti Québécois (PQ) was in power from 1976 to 1985 and ensured French-language dominance in Québec with Bill 101, alarming the province's Anglophone minority.

### Oui ou Non?

In 1995, the PQ held the second referendum on whether Québec should split from Canada. The "no" side won with 50.5 percent of the vote. Despite the narrow defeat, support for separatism has now dwindled.

## Top 10 Monuments

### 1 Place Royale

In 1642 settlers built a stockade where Montréal was founded (see p34).

### 2 Croix du Parc du Mont-Royal

The Sieur de Maisonneuve erected a cross in 1643 after the Ville-Marie settlement survived floods (see p8).

### 3 De Maisonneuve Monument

The Sieur de Maisonneuve ambushed by Iroquois stands at Place d'Armes. ◈ Map K2

### 4 Nelson Monument

Controversially erected in 1809 to celebrate victory over the French at the Battle of Trafalgar. ◈ Place Jacques-Cartier • Map L3

### 5 Brother André

A bronze monument commemorates the founder of the Oratoire St-Joseph (see pp10–11). ◈ Blvd Réne-Lévesque Ouest • Map H2

### 6 La Foule Illuminée

This sculpture by Raymond Masson fronts the Banque Nationale de Paris. ◈ Avenue McGill College • Map J1

### 7 James McGill

A monument to the university's founder. ◈ Avenue McGill College • Map J1

### 8 Monument George-Étienne Cartier

Montréal's largest monument is the setting for the popular Tam-Tam Festival (see p9).

### 9 Wolfe-Montcalm Monument

Commemorating the French and English generals. ◈ Parc des Gouverneurs • Map L5

### 10 Jardins Jeanne d'Arc

An equestrian memorial of the French heroine is surrounded by gardens. ◈ Map J6

Left **Place Jacques-Cartier** Right **Château Ramezay**

# 🔟 Historic Sites

### 1 Basilique Notre-Dame, Montréal

Once the largest church in North America, the imposing Gothic towers of the cathedral loom over Place d'Armes. Inside, a decorative nave is composed of stained-glass windows, hand-carved wooden statues, ornate goldleaf trimmings and paintings *(see pp12–13)*.

### 2 La Citadelle, Québec City

The colossal fortification was originally built by Royal Engineer Dubois Berthelet de Beaucours in 1693. The complete star-shaped bastion seen today however is primarily the work of English Colonel Elias Durnford, constructed between 1820 and 1832 *(see pp22–3)*.

### 3 Marché Bonsecours, Montréal

This beautiful Neo-Classical domed structure was once home to Canada's parliament but is today used variously as a produce market, art gallery,

concert venue, reception hall and shopping mall. The symmetrically designed gem of Vieux-Montréal features a Greek Revival portico and cast-iron columns made in the early 1800s *(see p56)*.

### 4 Place Royale, Montréal

Montréal's oldest public square (1657) is located on the site where the city was originally founded in 1642. It features the Pointe-à-Callière museum *(see pp18–19)*, a gift shop and outdoor events. The residence of Louis-Hector Callière, a French governor, was also once located here, as was the 19th-century Royal Insurance Building and Montréal's first Customs House. ⚓ *Map K3*

### 5 Place Jacques-Cartier, Montréal

The magnetic center of Vieux-Montréal, this square offers a variety of stores, clubs and restaurants, whilst being enlivened by street performers and horsedrawn *calèche* rides.

This is a wonderful spot to arrange meetings, take breaks from sightseeing, sit in the sun with a good book or simply people-watch. Look out for an entertaining troupe called the Old Montréal Ghost Trail located just south of the square, who offer tours of the city's eerier past *(see p55)*.

**Marché Bonsecours**

34

### 6 Hôtel de Ville, Montréal

While visiting Montréal's World Fair in 1967, French president Charles de Gaulle made history from the balcony of this building by announcing *"Vive le Québec – Vive le Québec Libre!"* ("Long Live Québec – Long Live Free Québec"), proving his support for the province's separation from the rest of Canada *(see p25)*. Sign up for a guided tour to fully enjoy the grace of this historic town hall *(see p56)*.

### 7 Château Ramezay, Montréal

An elegant heritage museum sits across the street from the Hôtel de Ville in an 18th-century former governor's home. Artifacts from Aboriginal societies through to the arrival of British and French colonizers up to 1900 are on display. The gift shop has unique souvenirs and the comfortable café terrace faces onto the Jardins du Gouverneur and Place Jacques-Cartier *(see p56)*.

Victorian clock, Sir George-Étienne-Cartier National Historic Site

### 8 Sir George-Etienne-Cartier National Historic Site, Montréal

A Victorian home, restored by Parks Canada as a National Historic Site, contains marvelous interactive exhibitions inviting visitors into a typical 19th-century parlor. Enjoy theatrical re-enactments portrayed in shows such as "A Victorian Christmas," "A Servant Confides," and "Elegance and Propriety: Etiquette at the Cartiers," all of which offer a fascinating insight into the lives once lived here *(see p57)*.

### 9 Parc des Champs-de-Bataille, Québec City

This park is a commemoration of the Battle of the Plains of Abraham, in which the generals of both sides, English General Wolfe and French General Montcalm, died during a fierce engagement lasting only 30 minutes *(see p32)*. The element of surprise was on the side of the British as no army had ever before managed to scale the Cap Diamant escarpment. A visit Maison de la Découverte (Discovery Pavilion) at 835 rue Wilfrid-Laurier will explain more on this important event and its resulting effect on Canadian history *(see p89)*.

### 10 Château Frontenac, Québec City

The most photographed hotel in the world poses majestically on the heights of Haute-Ville. Built by railroad tycoon Cornelius Van Horne, this elegant château was the first hotel to belong to the Canadian Pacific railroad empire *(see p112)*.

Château Frontenac

Left **Parc du Mont-Royal** Right **Parc des Champs-de-Bataille**

# Parks and Waterways

### 1 Parc du Mont-Royal, Montréal

The largest and most inviting natural playground in Montréal is loved passionately by residents. A year-round magnet for outdoor sports enthusiasts as well as leisure and relaxation buffs, Parc du Mont-Royal also boasts a wealth of wildlife and bird species, as well as a lake, streams, hiking paths, summer cycling and winter cross-country skiing trails, lookouts, an interpretation center and a wonderful collection of original sculptures *(see pp8–11)*.

### 2 Parc Maisonneuve, Montréal

Situated within the Parc Olympique area *(see pp14–17)*, these 60 acres of greenery provide fun and leisure in the east of the city. Facilities here include a 9-hole golf course in summer and a winter ice-skating rink that is floodlit at night. ✪ *Métro Viau*

### 3 Parc Lafontaine, Montréal

On the site of an old military armament range, attractive tree-lined pathways and shady spots are a perfect setting for many cultural events, celebrations and community activities throughout the year. The park is a friendly neighborhood expanse containing a duck pond, cultural center, concert venue and monuments honoring Québécois figures such as Félix Leclerc. ✪ *Map E2*

### 4 Pôle-des-Rapides

This historic area originated from the drama of the Lachine Rapids, which prevented early explorers, settlers, traders and the military from continuing farther west. It now includes the communities of Lachine, LaSalle and Verdun, minutes from downtown Montréal. Boasting the most popular cycle path in Canada and 100 km (60 miles) of trails, the district is also home to the Lachine National Historic Fur Trading Museum. ✪ *Map P6*

### 5 Parc Jean-Drapeau, Montréal

Parc Jean-Drapeau is made up of Ile Sainte-Hélène and Ile Notre-Dame. Most visitors come here to attend the amusement park or the numerous festivals and fireworks displays held throughout the year. ✪ *Map F5*

**Fireworks display, Parc Jean-Drapeau**

Place du Canada

### 6 Square Dorchester and Place du Canada, Montréal

This gracious square was the Catholic cemetery from 1798 to 1854 and is surrounded by elegant churches and buildings. Highlighted by the Sun Life Building on its east side, once the largest structure in the British Commonwealth, Square Dorchester contains numerous monuments, including one of the first French Canadian prime minister Sir Wilfrid Laurier, and is the starting point for city tours. Place du Canada was established to commemorate the nation's war dead from both World Wars. ✎ Map H2

### 7 Parc des Champs-de-Bataille, Québec City

The city's largest and most picturesque park. With over 250 acres of undulating hills and the St Lawrence River on the horizon, it's hard to believe that beautiful Battlefields Park has such a harsh military history. It was the site of the famed Battle of the Plains of Abraham in 1759, the events of which formed British Canada (see p89).

### 8 Parc Cavalier du Moulin, Québec City

At the western end of rue Mont-Carmel sits a delightful park, where poets, lovers and tourists enjoy the remarkable view of avenue Sainte-Geneviève, the Chalmers-Wesley United Church, Hôtel du Parlement, La Citadelle and the striking houses on rue Saint-Louis. ✎ Map L5

### 9 Parc de la Francophonie, Québec City

Created to commemorate the cultural alliance of 50 French-speaking countries, this peaceful park, with its ponds and fountains, is in stark contrast to the politically active area in which it lies, right beside the parliament building. This historic area was formerly known as Quartier St-Louis. ✎ Map K6

Parc de la Francophonie

### 10 Parc Montmorency, Québec City

At this magnificent vantage point, overlooking the St Lawrence River, Alfred Laliberté, a Montréal sculptor, has created bronze memorials to many famous Canadians, including one of Sir George-Étienne Cartier, whose signature is on the Confederation Act of 1867. From here there are great views of the Séminaire de Québec. ✎ Map M5

Left **Mordecai Richler** Right **Celine Dion with René Angelil**

# [TOP 10] Cultural Québécois

### Gabrielle Roy

Born in Manitoba to a French mother, and the youngest of 11 children, Roy (1909–83) escaped her family's poverty and moved to Québec in 1939, where she began her career as a respected and prolific French-speaking novelist. Her first work, *Bonheur d'occasion (The Tin Flute)*, was published in 1945, winning her the Prix Fémina award and the first of three coveted Governor General's awards.

### Émile Nelligan

Nelligan (1879–1941) was a romantic figurehead who ushered French-Canadian poetry into a new epoch and is revered by Quebecers as their beloved literary spokesmen. In 1897 Nelligan joined the École Littéraire de Montréal and caused a triumphant public reaction to the reading of his poem "La Romance du Vin." In later years Nelligan's sanity deteriorated and he spent his last days in an asylum.

**Émile Nelligan**

### Mary Travers

Travers (1894–1941), born to an impoverished family on the Gaspé Peninsula, was a natural entertainer and began her career at family soirées playing jigs on the fiddle and spoons. Known as "La Bolduc," she rose during the Great Depression to become the first popular singer-songwriter from Québec. A new generation of Quebecers has recently discovered her musical traditions.

### Paul-Émile Borduas

The painter Borduas (1905–60) is one of Québec's most legendary artists and also one of its greatest political activists. Born in St-Hilaire, just outside Montréal, he made his name when he criticized the established social and political norms in 1948 by writing a scathing manifesto entitled *Refus Global*. He was a founding member of the abstract Automatistes school of art, which eventually included Jean-Paul Riopelle.

### Félix Leclerc

Leclerc (1914–88) worked as a radio announcer, actor and comedian, but he is best remembered as a consummate storyteller, singer and songwriter, penning works about the Canadian countryside, solitude, and love. His monument is found on Ile d'Orléans, and a statue of him has been erected in his honor in Parc Lafontaine in Montreal (see p36).

### Robert Lepage

The first North American to direct a Shakespeare play at London's Royal National Theatre, Lepage (b.1957) is one of the most successful and daring writer/directors in the visual arts world. He has won every available Canadian award for his brilliant theatrical staging and continues to expand his creativity as a filmmaker.

### Cirque du Soleil

This circus troupe began life as street performers in La Malbaie, east of Québec City. Using an inventive mixture of world music, acrobatic brilliance and dazzling costumes, these entertainers have now conquered the world with their unique brand of magic. There are performance sites in Montréal, Las Vegas and Florida.

Oscar Peterson

### Oscar Peterson

Peterson (1925–2007) entered an amateur talent contest aged 14 in his home town Montréal – an event that he went on to win and which inspired him to leave high school and dedicate his life to jazz. However he was only given permission to do so by his father providing he worked to be the best jazz pianist in the world. Peterson succeeded beyond anyone's imagination: five unequalled decades of recordings are a testament to his virtuosity and have made him one of the greats of this musical genre.

### Mordecai Richler

The Montréal novelist, essayist and critic (1931–2001) was known for his sarcastic wit and biting opposition to Québec's separatist elements. His most popular book, *The Apprenticeship of Duddy Kravitz* (1959), was adapted for film, launching Richard Dreyfuss to Hollywood stardom in 1974. Richler is best known for writing about greed and the human condition, as in *St Urbain's Horseman* (1971) and *Barney's Version* (1998) but he also wrote a number of humorous essays.

Cirque du Soleil juggler

### Celine Dion

Dion (b.1968) is one of 14 children born into a musical family in Charlemagne. A demo tape made as a 12-year-old led to an agent, René Angelil, a recording contract and eventually to her and Angelil's marriage. Today she enjoys vast popularity as one of the world's finest singers.

To find out more about touring Cirque du Soleil performances, visit their website at www.cirquedusoleil.com

Left **Place des Arts** Right **Théâtre Petit Champlain**

# Performing Arts Venues

**Théâtre de Quat'Sous**

## 1 Théâtre de Quat'Sous, Montréal

Set in a former synagogue, this brilliant French troupe has given many young performers, writers and producers their first platform and so has established a loyal audience keen to appreciate new works. ◈ 100 ave des Pins Est • Map D3 • (514) 845 7277 • www.quatsous.com

## 2 Théâtre d'Aujourd'hui, Montréal

A French theater company founded in 1968, committed to writing, staging and producing Québécois plays. It is guided by the passion of artistic director Marie-Thérèse Fortin. ◈ 3900 rue St-Denis • Map E2 • (514) 282 3900

## 3 Théâtre du Nouveau Monde, Montréal

Begun in 1951, this is the heart of Québécois theater. The company moved to this heritage building in 1972 and has put on legendary shows ever since. ◈ 84 rue Ste-Catherine Ouest • Map K1 • (514) 866 8668

## 4 Place des Arts, Montréal

This is the cultural center-piece of Montréal. Five modern venues and an outdoor plaza house countless performances and are permanent homes to the Orchestre symphonique de Montréal, Opéra Montréal and the Grands Ballets Canadiens de Montréal. It is also the seasonal home of the International Jazz Festival of Montréal, Festival Francofolies and Festival Montréal en lumière (see pp42–3). ◈ Map K1 • (514) 842 2112 • www.pdarts.com

## 5 Centaur Theatre, Montréal

Montréal's principal English-language theatrical venue was founded in 1969. Housed in the Old Stock Exchange Building, it has two stages and is fast becoming known for its world-class productions. The program varies between Broadway musicals, contemporary Canadian drama, as well as works by international playwrights, past and present. ◈ 453 rue St-François-Xavier • Map K3 • (514) 288 3161 • www.centaurtheatre.com

**Théâtre du Nouveau Monde**

### 6 Théâtre du Rideau Vert, Montréal

For over 50 years (established in 1949) this French-speaking theater has had an outstanding reputation for the quality of its productions. Everything from classics to contemporary works to international tours. 🔊 *4664 rue St-Denis • Map E2 • (514) 844 1793 • www.rideauvert.qc.ca*

### 7 Théâtre du Petit Champlain Maison de la Chanson, Québec City

Perhaps the most compelling new theater in the country is hidden on a crowded stretch of the rue du Petit Champlain. The building is a beautiful example of fusing history with contemporary design; inside, the performance space is comfortable and the audience seating generous. The schedule has up-and-coming acts as well as established artists. 🔊 *68–78 rue du Petit Champlain • Map M5 • (418) 692 2631 • www.theatrepetitchamplain.com*

### 8 Le Capitole de Québec et Cabaret du Capitole, Québec City

Le Capitole is a testament to the committed preservation of historic buildings in Québec City. Built in 1903 and refurbished by New York architect Thomas W. Lamb in the 1920s, it was given a third lease on life in the 1980s and is now the preferred showcase for theater, cabaret and cultural events. Also on site are a restaurant, a chic bar and a luxury hotel. 🔊 *972 rue St-Jean • Map K5 • (418) 694 4444 • www.lecapitole.com*

### 9 Grand Théâtre de Québec, Québec City

Conceived by Canadian architect and urban theorist Victor Prus, this inventive space uses a stacked concert hall grid to

Le Capitole de Québec

maximize on space limitations. The theater opened in 1971 and features a spectacular mural by Québec artist Jordi Bonet, which leads to the Salle Louis-Fréchette and Octave-Crémazie concert halls. Théâtre Trident, Opéra de Québec and the Club musical de Québec are based here, as well as concerts by the Orchestre symphonique de Québec. Pop concerts by international artists are also staged here sometimes. 🔊 *269 blvd René-Lévesque Est • Map H6 • (418) 643 8131 • www.grandtheatre.qc.ca*

### 10 Théâtre de la Bordée, Québec City

After staging over 100 productions in temporary digs, the French-speaking Théâtre de la Bordée troupe has finally found its own home, in the refurbished Pigalle movie house in the Quartier St-Roch. Under the influence of artistic director Luc Robitaille the company is inviting luminaries such as Robert Lepage *(see p39)* to mount original works. 🔊 *315 rue St-Joseph Est • Map K5 • (418) 694 9721 • www.bordee.qc.ca*

Left **Motor racing** Right **Le Festival International de Jazz de Montréal**

# Festivals and Events

### 1 Motor racing in Montréal
Montréal's two annual motor races draw thousands of visitors from across the world. They are held at the Circuit Gilles-Villeneuve, named after the French-Canadian racing driver.

### 2 Le Festival International de Jazz de Montréal
The world's largest jazz festival takes over the concourse at Place des Arts in downtown Montréal, as well as neighborhood clubs, restaurants and parks. Each year several million visitors party for 11 days of free outdoor concerts and a wide variety of musical events involving internationally renowned musicians. ◈ Late Jun–Jul; www.montrealjazzfest.com

### 3 L'International des Feux Loto-Québec
From mid-June to the end of July the skies over Old Montréal light up twice a week with explosive theatrics. Held at La Ronde amusement park (see p47), countries from around the world display their pyrotechnic talents. ◈ Wed & Sat: 10pm; www.international desfeuxloto-quebec.com

### 4 Just For Laughs Festival
Over 1.5 million jolly patrons attend a banquet of mirth each year in July at Montréal's comedy festival. From quirky free shows in Quartier Latin streets to the constantly sold-out Club Series and Loto-Québec Galas, humor in all its forms is on offer from more than 600 international performers. ◈ www.hahaha.com

### 5 Les FrancoFolies de Montréal
A wildly eclectic music festival celebrating all French music. Over 500,000 people attend concerts by groups far from the mainstream of North American culture, with styles ranging from hip-hop to creole, rap, swing and, of course, traditional French songs. ◈ Late Jul–Aug; www.francofolies.com

### 6 Festival Montréal en Lumière
The spirits of Montrealers are given a boost during the winter months in this celebration of life through light. Each night over the

**Festival Montréal en Lumière**

For the most popular festivals, such as the Montréal jazz festival, the city becomes very crowded, so book hotels well in advance.

**Festival d'Été**

settling of the city by the French in the 1600s *(see p32)*. Early August crowds are invited to attend over 600 performances by local actors, musicians, dancers and artists. It's not all about history – there is also a generous element of fun, including games, competitions and concerts. ✆ *www. nouvellefrance.qc.ca*

festival's two-week run in February, organizers host a wild combination of attractions, from outdoor light and music *(son et lumière)* productions, to indoor concerts, illuminated buildings, theatre and dance performances, culinary soirées of traditional foods, and nightly fireworks. This is a spectacular time in the city. ✆ *www.montrealhighlights.com*

### Festival d'Été de Québec

For 10 explosive days each July, Québec City becomes one mammoth outdoor music stage as performers flock from all over the world to perform countless styles of music for the enthusiastic crowds. This enormous spectacle is the most spirited activity of the summer with 500 shows and some 1,000 artists blasting out their sounds at over 15 different performance venues. ✆ *www.infofestival.com*

### Fêtes de la Nouvelle-France

A large-scale voyage back in time transforms Place Royale and the Basse-Ville section of Québec City into a magical *mélange* of period costumes, traditional music and dance, and authentic foods, all to celebrate the

### Festival International des Arts Traditionaux

A superb multicultural festival each fall at Chapelle du Musée de l'Amérique française in Vieux-Québec *(see p24)* offers a sensuous feast of traditional music, dance, crafts, foods and laughter. Share homespun hilarity while watching teams joust during *Joute chantée* (an improvised singing tournament), or during the culinary fun of *Souper chanté* (singing supper). Singers come from as far afield as Guatemala, Japan, Greece, Martinique and Senegal.

### Tournoi International de Hockey Pee-Wee de Québec

Each February, the largest youth hockey tournament in the world brings over 100 teams from more than a dozen countries to face off against each other in Québec's Colisée arena. More than 644 players have had professional hockey careers after playing in this tournament, including Wayne Gretzky. The building itself is called "the house Jean Béliveau built" by locals, referring to the ice hockey legend who once played here. ✆ *www.tournoipee-wee.qc.ca*

 *For details of Carnaval de Québec* **See pp44–5**

Left **Hôtel de Glace** Right **International Snow Sculpture Competition**

# 🔟 Carnaval de Québec Attractions

### 1 Palais de Glace
The anticipation grows throughout Québec City each February as the winter carnival organization builds its captivating Ice Palace. Over 6,000 frozen blocks of ice are sculpted by an army of artisans into a dreamy castle, complete with turrets, drawbridge, and a stage for a sound and light show. Québec's magnificent temporary monument to winter sits appropriately across from the most serious edifice in the area – the Parliament Buildings.

### 2 Bonhomme Carnaval
The symbol of Québec's innovative winter fête is a character who appeals to the kids – a large jolly snowman dressed up for a party. Bonhomme Carnaval, with his signature red sash and wooly hat, has been the international icon of this frozen extravaganza for 50 years, calling children and

**Bonhomme Carnaval**

the young-at-heart everywhere to free themselves from winter's frozen grasp, bundle up in warm attire and join him to celebrate life in his frigid surroundings.

### 3 Place de la Famille
Set on the expansive Plains of Abraham, Québec's Winter Carnival team of 1,500 volunteers builds a fantasyland of ice and snow. Designers assemble a range of energy-filled games and contests across the city's landscape that keep body temperatures high, no matter what the thermometer outside is reading.

### 4 International Snow Sculpture Competition
The most famous of all the events during Carnaval. Competitors from around the globe arrive to first rough-sculpt the ice with chain saws then delicately chisel away to form amazing designs. Some of the contestants, such as those

**Palais de Glace**

*The Carnaval de Québec takes place over two weeks each February.*

from the Caribbean, have never seen snow before, adding to the humorous interaction between the teams and the audiences.

### 5 Ski Competition
Outside the city limits, the fun continues with more serious winter sports. Downhill and cross-country skiing competitions are held in the Jacques-Cartier area of Lac Beauport, 20 minutes from Québec City.

### 6 St. Hubert's Snow Bath
Goosebumps abound at this zany Plains of Abraham demonstration. Teams of snow bathers dressed only in bathing suits compete to see which team can conquer the freezing exposure by lying in the snow. Onlookers of every age are guaranteed laughs, as 75 courageous men and women brave the cold.

### 7 Hôtel de Glace
Unique in North America and only the second in the world, the Ice Hotel (see p101) fits perfectly into the line-up for Québec's Winter Carnaval. Located in the Duchesnay Ecotourism Centre, 30 minutes outside the city, the Ice Hotel offers Carnaval participants a spectacular architectural stay. Explore the themed bedrooms, Absolut Vodka bar, wedding chapel and ice sculptures. ✆ www.icehotel-canada.com

### 8 La Parade
Every evening of Carnaval two parades mark the end of the day's festivities. The "Little (But Loud) Parade" is for adults, while "La petite fanfare du Bonhomme" gathers momentum throughout the Place de la Famille creating a ceremonial end to the day for children.

Les Glissades de la Terrasse Dufferin

### 9 Carnaval Refreshments
Ever since the French settled Québec they have traditionally celebrated with food, wine and song just before the Catholic period of Lent, a time when religious customs suggest abstaining from alcohol and other temptations. Be prepared for locals to offer you the infamous mixture Caribou, a hot alcoholic drink containing brandy, vodka, sherry, port and sometimes maple sugar. Watch it – it's as potent as it sounds.

### 10 Les Glissades de la Terrasse Dufferin
The panoramic splendor of this slope beside Château Frontenac (see p93) is the customary location for the world's most scenic winter slide. If visitors refrain from participating in other Québec Winter Carnaval activities, happy to be just a spectator of all the fun, they should make an exception with this ride. Each year the organizers seem to build a better slide and with the St Lawrence River spread out before you, it is a beautiful and exhilarating experience.

Left **Insectarium** Right **Biodôme**

# 🔟 Children's Attractions

### Insectarium, Montréal
This astounding display celebrates insects of every size and
shape. It opened in 1990 thanks
to Georges Brossard, who
traveled the world to collect the
fascinating bugs. Although most
of the insects are dead, there are
live tarantulas and other creepy
crawlies, safely ensconced
behind glass *(see p15)*. ✎ *4581 rue
Sherbrooke Est • Métro Pie-IX • (514)
872 1400 • Open daily (times vary) • Adm
• www.ville.montreal.qc.ca/insectarium*

### Biodôme, Montréal
It is rare to see birds from
the northern and southern hemi-
spheres in one place, but in this
unusual exhibit animals from
the Arctic, Antarctic, Tropics,
Laurentian and St Lawrence
marine habitats are housed

**Statue fronting the Planetarium**

under one roof in a controlled
setting resembling their natural
surroundings *(see p14)*. ✎ *4777 ave
Pierre-de-Coubertin • Métro Viau • (514)
868 3000 • Open 9am–4pm daily • Adm
• www.ville.montreal.qc.ca/biodome*

### Planetarium, Montréal
Under the starry skies
projected onto the Star Theatre's
domed ceiling, visitors are pro-
pelled into the heavens courtesy
of high-precision technology. A
fascinating journey into time and
outer space to fathom the planets
and the universe. ✎ *1000 rue St-
Jacques Ouest • Métro Bonaventure
• (514) 872 4530 • Opening times vary
• Adm • www.planetarium.montreal.qc.ca*

### La Ronde Six Flags Amusement Park, Montréal
The largest amusement park in
Québec was originally opened
for Expo '67. Since Six Flags
took over as owner in 2001,
however, even more fun can be
had as new rides and attractions

**La Ronde Six Flags Amusement Park**

*Sign up for DK's email newsletter on traveldk.com*

are added each year. Enthusiasts will love Vertigo, which swings visitors 18 m (60 ft) up in the air through a 360-degree rotation. Tamer rides, such as spinning tea cups and carousels, will appeal to younger children. ◈ *22 chemin MacDonald, Ile Ste-Hélène • Map F4 • (514) 397 2000 • Open May–Oct: daily • Adm • www.laronde.com*

### Laser Quest, Montréal
This exciting adventure involves making your way around a dark labyrinth of passageways equipped with a laser beam with which you score points by zapping other participants. The journey is accompanied by rousing music, which only adds to the atmosphere. ◈ *1226 rue Ste-Catherine Ouest • Map G1 • (514) 393 3000 • Open 5pm–9pm Wed–Thu, 4pm–11pm Fri, noon–11pm Sat, noon–7pm Sun; Mon–Tue for private groups only • Adm*

Learning center, Centre des Sciences

### Centre des Sciences de Montréal
The underlying thrust of this compelling center (also known as iSci) is to demystify all aspects of science, from technology and how it influences our daily lives, to exploring the underwater world of the ocean. Entertaining and innovative interactive games make the learning fun. For younger kids there is an indoor playground with a model dragon *(see p58)*. ◈ *www.centredesscciencesdemontreal.com*

### Le Théâtre de L'Oeil, Montréal
Performances, workshops and exhibitions are all part of the fun at this puppet theater. Kids can watch how the puppets are made, learn to pull strings, and attend a show. ◈ *7780 Henri-Julien Ave • Map E1 • (514) 278 9188 • Open 10am–6pm Tue–Sun • Adm • www.theatredeloeil.qc.ca*

### CinéRobothèque, Montréal
Choose a film from the National Film Board's inventory, then watch while a robot goes through its routines to find, select and deliver the video to you without error. Then enjoy the film in a private viewing unit. ◈ *1564 rue St-Denis • Map L1 • (514) 496 6887*

### Labyrinthe du Hangar 16, Montréal
Each year a tantalizing new theme is created to lure young people into an intricate maze of corridors, obstacles, puzzles, surprises and thrills, in this port hangar. The entire family can solve the mysteries together, or kids can go on their own. ◈ *Quai de l'Horloge (Clock Tower Pier) • Map M3 • (514) 499 0099 • Open daily • Adm*

### Cosmodôme, Laval
A fascinating look at space and the universe in all its diversity. Large scale models of the solar system explain the make-up of every planet, while the rockets exhibition provides an insight into space travel. ◈ *2150 Laurentian Autoroute, Laval • (450) 978 3600 • Open 10am–6pm Tue–Sun (daily Jul–Aug) • Adm • www.cosmodome.org*

Left **Whitewater Rafting** Right **Cycling the Piste du P'tit Train du Nord**

# 🔟 Outdoor Activities

### 1 Boating, Canoeing and Rafting

These activities have always been an integral part of life in Montréal. Yachts and sailboats contribute to the colorful marine ambiance of the Vieux-Port in Montréal. Saute-Moutons is the premier Lachine Rapids jetboat (motorized rafting) excursion, departing from the Quai de l'Horloque, while canoeing can be enjoyed on the Canal Lachine. ⊗ *Jetboat excursions: 47 rue de la Commune Ouest; (514) 284 9607; www.jetboatingmontreal.com*

### 2 Downhill Skiing

There are hundreds of skiing trails throughout the Laurentian, Adirondack, Green and White Mountain ranges within hours of both cities. For Montréalers, the Cantons de l'Est offer pistes at Mont Orford *(see pp84–5)*, while Québec City enthusiasts have runs at Massif and Mont Sainte-Anne *(see p100)*.

### 3 Cross Country Skiing

Cross-country legends abound in Québec, with Herman "Jackrabbit" Johannsen *(see p31)* leading the list of adventurers. In Montréal it is possible to enjoy cross-country skiing in many parks, with locals favoring Parc du Cap Saint-Jacques because of its 900-acre domain.

### 4 Piste du P'tit Train du Nord

A former rail track has now been turned into a 200-km (125-mile) hiking, cycling and cross-country ski trail. The train once took weekenders to the Laurentian mountains from Montréal at the southern end to Mont-Laurier on the northern extreme. ⊗ *Map N5*

### 5 Swimming

There are more than 30 indoor pools in the Montréal area, including Olympic-size facilities at Parc Olympique *(see pp14–15)*. In summer there is a beach on Ile Notre-Dame, south of Vieux-Port.

### 6 Skating and Snowshoeing

Indoor arenas in summer and outdoor city parks and lakes in winter provide numerous ice-skating options in both cities, while snowshoeing is reserved for larger tracts of land such as Parc du Mont-Royal in Montréal.

**Skating in front of Château Frontenac, Québec City**

Mountain climbing

## Rapelling and Mountain Climbing

These are two of the fastest growing adventure sports throughout Québec, with a bevy of challenges available outside both cities. The vast mountainous expanses are overseen by Sépaq (Parks Québec). ✆ *Sépaq: 1-800 665 6527* • *www.sepaq.com*

## Dogsledding

Winter dogsled trips are a fantastic way of becoming one with nature as packs of huskies pull you through the forests of the province. Contact Sépaq for more information. ✆ *1-800 665 6527*

## Horse Riding

Immediately west of Montréal is horse country. Visitors can make a day of it by touring the rolling hills of Hudson and Rigaud (see p81) and be back in the city by nightfall. The Double J Ranch also has a network of trails. ✆ *Double J Ranch: (450) 455 7075*

## Fishing and Hunting

Wildlife abounds for hunters in Québec, whether searching for white-tailed deer, moose, caribou or pheasant. The fishing here has long attracted the rich and famous; it offers some of the best river salmon fishing in the world. ✆ *Fishing & Hunting trips: 1-800 567 5191* • *www.fpq.com*

---

## Top 10 Spectator Sports

### 1 Les Canadiens de Montréal Club de Hockey
One of the world's most successful professional sports organizations attracts 800,000 fans to the Molson Center.

### 2 Tournoi International de Hockey Pee-Wee de Quebec
The largest youth hockey tournament in the world.

### 3 Motor Racing in Montréal
The planet's fastest drivers tour the Circuit Gilles-Villeneuve in Montréal's two annual motor races (see p42).

### 4 Red Bull Crashed Ice Tournament
Competitors strap on skates and pads to race down an ice track with spectacular crashes.

### 5 Tour de l'Ile de Montréal
The entire city turns out for this 65-km (40-mile) bicycle race.

### 6 Montréal Alouettes Canadian Football
Winner of the 2002 Grey Cup, the Montréal Alouettes play at the Percival Molson Stadium.

### 7 Montréal Impact Soccer
Montréal's Impact is the city's main soccer team.

### 8 Parc Jarry Tennis Championships
International professional tennis competitions are held at Parc Jarry.

### 9 Montréal Air Show
Each May, pilots stage a show of synchronized flying and daredevil acrobatics.

### 10 Montréal Marathon
Every September hundreds of runners take part in this race through the city.

Left **Chez Maurice Nightclub Complex** Right **Montréal nightlife**

# Nightclubs and Casinos

### Casino de Montréal
The most stunning casino in Canada, given its location on the Ile Notre-Dame and overlooking the Vieux-Port and the glittering towers of downtown. The casino offers a full house of attractions including four superb dining facilities and nightly variety shows. Over 18s only. ◈ *1 ave du Casino, Ile Notre-Dame • Map E6 • Open daily • Free • www.casinosduquebec.com/montreal*

### Altitude 737, Montréal
Using its height as its moniker, with views over Mont-Royal and the St Lawrence River valley, this three-floor enterprise offers visitors an entertainment package of lounge, dance club and restaurant. In summer they open the spectacular terrace for additional dancing space. Reservations recommended. ◈ *1 Place Ville Marie, 42nd Floor • Map J2 • (514) 397 0737 • www.altitude737.com*

### Le Belmont, Montréal
Le Belmont has established itself as a landmark bar with the student crowd as well as office workers looking to unwind on the large dance-floor. Brick walls, pool tables and beer on tap create a welcoming atmosphere in the first area, while the larger dance club has more space and DJ-spun house music. ◈ *4483 blvd St-Laurent • Map D2 • (514) 845 8443*

### Au Diable Vert, Montréal
If drinking, dancing and partying with the artists and students of Montréal's Plateau area sounds like a good idea then head for this pub. The city's most danceable DJs work the floor each weekend, while during the week the ambiance is more laid-back. Great beers and an amiable clientele. ◈ *4557 rue St-Denis • Map E1 • (514) 849 5888 • www.audiablevert.net*

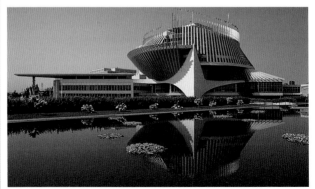

**Casino de Montréal**

### Upstairs Jazz Club, Montréal

Providing the best jazz music in Montréal is not simple in a city that annually hosts the world's largest jazz festival (see p42). But with a tenacious attention to detail and atmosphere, as well as mixing international and local musicians, the owners of this popular club have succeeded in their aim. There's a changing program of entertainment and delicious food served, too. Cover charge. ✪ *1254 rue MacKay • Map G1 • (514) 931 6808 • www.upstairsjazz.com*

Upstairs Jazz Club

### Club Opera, Montréal

The ultimate dance club in Montréal, Club Opera attracts a continuous stream of international hip-hop performers and DJs to this central downtown site until the early hours of the morning. Volume rules in this massive space. Don't even think about turning up until after midnight when it is really thumping. Cover charge and open to over 18s only. ✪ *32 rue Ste-Catherine Ouest • Map K1*

### Chez Maurice Nightclub Complex, Québec City

A pulsating complex of nightlife temptations awaits the nocturnal patrons of this hugely popular Québec City club. Housing five dynamic areas, over three floors, the main attraction is the massive (and very loud) dance floor, filled with chic and beautiful 20- to 35-year-olds who have been carefully hand-picked by the doormen from a constant line-up outside. The top-floor lounge, Chez Charlotte, has a spectacular terrace that can seat up to 500 people, or try the Voodoo Grill for gourmet munchies. Cover charge. Over 18s only (see p97).

### Palais Montcalm, Québec City

This elegant multi-room venue regularly draws the biggest names in Canadian and international music. A smaller, more intimate café-style room, the Café-spectacles, offers music from emerging blues and jazz artists (see p97).

### L'Impérial de Québec

This concert venue, set in a 19th-century theatre, hosts top local and international artists as well as Broadway-style shows. The bistro serves good food, too. ✪ *252 rue St-Joseph Est • Map H4 • 1-877 523 3131 • www.imperialdequebec.com*

### Casino de Charlevoix

A breathtaking 90-minute drive northeast of Québec City along the north shore of the St Lawrence River and through the rugged Charlevoix region brings you to the majestic Fairmont Le Manoir Richelieu Hotel. Here US presidents, movie moguls and tourists of every background have come to relax in historic splendor. Expanded in 1994 to include a casino, the facility now offers 780 slot machines and 21 table games. ✪ *181 rue Richelieu, La Malbaie, Charlevoix • Map Q2 • 1-800 665 2274*

# AROUND MONTRÉAL & QUÉBEC CITY

MONTRÉAL & QUÉBEC CITY'S TOP 10

Left **Séminaire St-Sulpice** Right **Place Jacques-Cartier**

# Vieux-Montréal & Vieux-Port

THIS ENCHANTING AREA, ESTABLISHED IN 1642, *is the most rewarding spot to begin a tour of the city of Montréal. Its ancient churches, cobblestone streets, horse-drawn* calèches *and the bustling international port characterize this fascinating neighborhood. Vieux-Montréal epitomizes the romance, culture and* joie-de-vivre *of the metropolis, while the activity of mega-freighters and palatial cruise boats in the Vieux-Port reveals that Montréal is the shipping gateway to the Great Lakes. The old quarter combines high-tech novelty with old-world charm as well as some of the city's best dining options. Plan to spend several days exploring the craft shops, museums, cultural exhibitions and French bistros while savoring the European-style hospitality presented in a vivacious Québécois manner.*

## TOP 10 Sights

1. Basilique Notre-Dame
2. Musée Pointe-à-Callière
3. Séminaire St-Sulpice
4. Place Jacques-Cartier & Place de la Dauversière
5. Musée Marguerite-Bourgeoys & Chapelle Notre-Dame-de-Bon-Secours
6. Hôtel de Ville
7. Musée Château Ramezay
8. Marché Bonsecours
9. Sir George-Étienne-Cartier National Historic Site
10. Musée Marc-Aurèle Fortin

**Basilique Notre-Dame**

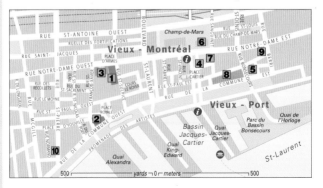

### Basilique Notre-Dame

When the largest bell in North America begins to thunder over Place d'Armes, legions of pigeons create a spectacle reminiscent of St Peter's Square in Rome. Meanwhile throngs of pilgrims and visitors flock daily to this compelling architectural masterpiece (see pp12–13).

### Musée Pointe-à-Callière

This striking modern building, married with the more ancient Place Royale setting, vibrates with activity throughout the year, as visitors digest one cultural exhibition treat after another on display inside and outside this museum (see pp18–19).

### Séminaire St-Sulpice

Erected between 1685 and 1687 as the home of the Sulpician religious order, the St Sulpice Seminary is the oldest surviving building in Montréal. This remarkable historic edifice remains an icon of the institutional architecture that was employed in Nouvelle-France. The Sulpicians' exterior clock above the main doorway is the oldest of its kind in North America, dating from 1701 (see p13). ✎ 116 rue Notre Dame Ouest • Map K3

### Place Jacques-Cartier & Place de la Dauversière

Two famous names in Canadian history have beautiful squares directly across from each other. Place Jacques-Cartier (see p34) celebrates the French discoverer of Canada (see p32), while Place de la Dauversière honors Jerome le Royer, Sieur de la Dauversière of La Flèche in Anjou, France. Dauversière was the Royal Tax Collector whose idea it was to build a colony here, eventually called Ville-Marie. ✎ Map L3

### Musée Marguerite-Bourgeoys & Chapelle Notre-Dame-de-Bon-Secours

In 1653 Marguerite Bourgeoys arrived in Ville-Marie to open a school, which began in a stable assigned to her by the Sieur de Maisonneuve. By 1655 she was head of the Congregation of the Sisters of Notre-Dame and oversaw the construction of Canada's first stone church in 1675. The chapel that remains dates from 1771. It is known as the "Sailors Chapel," given its portside location and model ships hanging throughout. ✎ 400 rue St-Paul Est • Map L3 • Open Mar–Apr: 11am–3:30pm Tue–Sun; May–Oct: 10am–5:30pm Tue–Sun; Nov–mid-Jan: 11am–3:30pm Tue–Sun • Adm • www.marguerite–bourgeoys.com

**Chapelle Notre-Dame-de-Bon-Secours**

*Because of the cobblestone streets in Vieux-Montréal, make sure you wear comfortable shoes while exploring.*

### The French Arrival and the Fur Trade

The original Huron village of Hochelaga (meaning "where the rivers meet") provided the French explorers with an ideal location from which to settle the new continent and the key staging area for exploration of the rest of North America. It also allowed access to the Huron fur-trading networks, resulting in an enormously profitable fur trade between Canada and Europe.

## 6 Hôtel de Ville

Montréal's town hall was a gracious Second Empire-style edifice built between 1872 and 1878 by architect Henri-Maurice Perrault (1828–1903). Damaged by fire in 1922 it was rebuilt a year later in Beaux-Arts style, inaugurated in 1926 and is still used for its original function. It is possible to visit the interior and City Council sessions, open to the public on Monday nights at 7pm. It offers one of the most extravagant sights each evening when its array of lights illuminate the night sky *(see p35)*. *275 rue Notre-Dame Est • Map L2 • Open 8am–5pm Mon–Fri • Free (adm for sessions)*

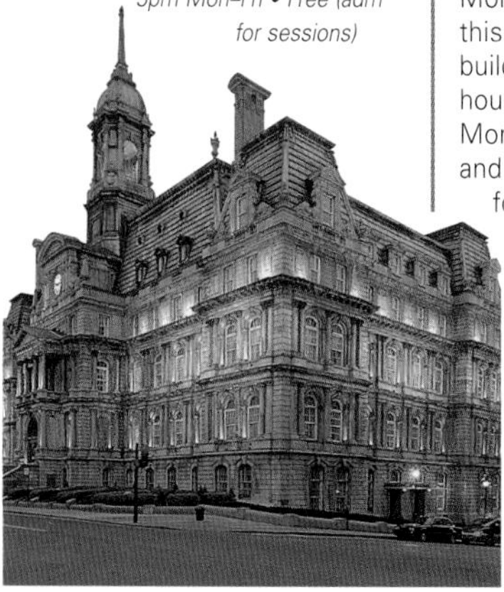

**Hôtel de Ville**

## 7 Musée Château Ramezay

This elegant stone home was originally constructed to house the Governor of Montréal, Claude de Ramezay (1659–1724) and his 16 children. Once the Ramezay family departed it was thereafter known as the Maison des Castors (beavers) because it was home to the Compagnie des Indes (West Indies Company) and their burgeoning fur trade with Europe. In 1775 General Richard Montgomery lived here with his band of rebellious Americans while they made a failed attempt to capture the city for the US. It has been a museum since 1895, with artifacts illustrating the early settlement of Québec, from tools to uniforms to historic documents. Of particular note is the Nantes Salon, lavishly decorated by 18th-century French architect, Germain Boffrand *(see p35)*. *280 rue Notre-Dame Est • Map L3 • (514) 861 3708 • Open Jun–Sep: 10am–6pm daily; Oct–May: 10am–4:30pm Tue–Sun • Dis. access • Adm • www.chateauramezay.qc.ca*

## 8 Marché Bonsecours

Built on the site of John Molson's British American Hotel, this greystone Neo-Classical building has a rich history. It once housed the Parliament of Canada, Montréal's temporary City Hall and was even a theatrical venue for Charles Dickens when he acted at the Theatre Royal in 1842. Today it is a smart shopping center, and its designer boutiques, art exhibitions and souvenir shops attract a continuing influx of visitors under its shining dome *(see p34)*. *350 rue St-Paul Est • Map L3 • Open Jun–Sep: 10am–9pm daily; Sep–Jun: 10am–6pm daily (to 9pm Thu & Fri)*

**Sir George-Étienne-Cartier House**

### Sir George-Étienne-Cartier National Historic Site

Exquisitely preserved artifacts of the 19th-century upper-middle-classes and their lifestyle are commemorated at Sir George-Étienne-Cartier's house, now a National Historic Site. Cartier was one of the Fathers of Canadian Confederation and his impeccable home, in which he lived from 1848 to 1871, provides an insight into the mores of his social class at that time. Using the Victorian decor as a backdrop for theatrical re-enactments, the on-site performing troupe enlivens the home and its detailed history *(see p35).* ◈ *458 rue Notre-Dame Est • Map L3 • Open Apr–mid-Jun & early Sep–Dec: 10am–5pm Wed–Sun; mid-Jun– early Sep: 10am–5:30pm daily • Adm*

### Musée Marc-Aurèle Fortin

Fortin (1888–1970) is regarded as one of the most influential landscape artists of the 20th century and his fluid portrayals of his native Québec Province, capturing its unique light, fill this tiny museum, which is housed in a former 19th-century stone warehouse. This is the largest permanent collection of his works in the world. Also on display are contemporary works by local artists. ◈ *118 rue St-Pierre • Map J3 • Open 11am–5pm Tue–Sun • Adm • www.museemafortin.org*

## A Morning Stroll along the Waterfront

🕐 Start your walk on rue St-Pierre at the **Musée Marc-Aurèle Fortin** to see his masterful paintings of Québec's countryside. There is an interesting plaque next door providing a history of the neighborhood buildings. Continue down St-Pierre towards the waterfront and cross rue de la Commune to the walking path. Turn right to inspect the locks then enter the pretty Parc des Écluses. The park's restaurant terrace is a perfect place for a morning coffee break.

Next, head east along the waterfront where you may find second-hand book-sellers, yachts of the rich and famous and portrait artists vying for your attention. Stay beside the water, past the **Centre des Sciences de Montréal** *(see p58)* to Bassin Bonsecours, the waterfall, **Quai de l'Horloge** *(see p58).*

Go north to the Chapelle Notre-Dame-de-Bonsecours *(400 rue St-Paul Est)* where, if you are feeling energetic, you can climb the interior stairs for a wonderful view of the Vieux-Port, then go directly across the street to **Auberge Pierre du Calvet** *(see p58).* Take a peek inside at the sumptuous period surroundings.

End your walk by strolling through **Marché Bonsecours** with its designer boutiques, then continue along rue St-Paul and buy a take-out lunch at **Resto Chez l'Epicier** *(see p63)* to enjoy on **Place Jacques-Cartier** *(see p55)* while people-watching.

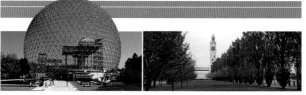

Left **Biosphère** Right **Quai de l'Horloge**

# Best of the Rest

### 1 Centre des Sciences de Montréal

This science and technology center (also known as iSci) offers quality entertainment for kids with its games, IMAX theater and interactive exhibits *(see p47)*. ✆ *Quai King-Edward • Map K3 • (514) 496 4724 • Open 9am–4pm Mon–Fri, 10am–5pm Sat–Sun • Dis. access • Adm*

### 2 Biosphère

An architectural centerpiece created for Expo '67, the dome now acts as an Ecowatch Centre and a museum dedicated to the St Lawrence River and Great Lakes. ✆ *160 rue Tour de l'Isle, Ile Ste-Hélène • Map F5 • (514) 283 5000 • Open 10am–6pm daily • Dis. access • Adm*

### 3 Auberge Pierre du Calvet

One of the most romantic spots in Montréal, this 1725 inn presents an outstanding collection of antiques. Dine in Les Filles du Roy restaurant for some delectable cuisine. ✆ *405 rue Bonsecours • Map L3 • (514) 282 1725*

### 4 Quai de l'Horloge

The 1922 clock tower still keeps time. Climb the interior stairs for a great view over the port. ✆ *Map M3*

### 5 Casino de Montréal

This sparkling casino includes musical variety shows, gourmet dining, 3,000 slot machines and 120 gaming tables *(see p50)*. ✆ *Ile Notre-Dame • Map E6 • Open 24 hours daily • Dis. access • Free*

### 6 Square Victoria

In 1860 a magnificent monument to honor Queen Victoria was erected on this haymarket square. ✆ *Map J2*

### 7 Centre d'Histoire de Montréal

This former firehall provides an interactive exhibition containing many local treasures of Montréal. ✆ *335 place d'Youville • Map K3 • Open mid-May–Aug: 10am–5pm daily; Sep–mid-May: 10am–5pm Tue–Sun • Adm*

### 8 Old Customs House

A classic example of 1830s architecture is today part of the Musée Pointe-à-Callière *(see p19)*.

### 9 Bank of Montréal Museum

The oldest bank in Canada (1817) houses an interesting currency museum within an ornate interior. ✆ *129 rue St-Jacques Ouest • Map K3 • Open 10am–4pm Mon–Fri • Free*

### 10 Stewart Museum at the Fort

Montréal's only fort invites tourists to explore over 400 years of military history. ✆ *20 rue Tour de l'Isle, Ile Ste-Hélène • Map F4 • Open 10am–5pm Wed–Mon • Adm*

Left **Centre du Commerce Mondial** Right **Souvenirs, Conseil des Métiers d'Art du Québec**

# 🔟 Shops

### Marché Bonsecours
A Vieux-Montréal heritage landmark is now a bustling area of designer boutiques *(see p56)*.

### Centre de Commerce Mondial
An inspiring architectural concept has been created by interlinking Ruelle des Fortifications heritage structures under a spectacular glass atrium. Shops, offices and a hotel are found here. 🔊 *747 square Victoria • Map J2 • Dis. access*

### Galerie Michel-Ange
A reliable art gallery featuring many fine Québécois and international painters, located in a heritage house built in 1864. 🔊 *430 rue Bonsecours • Map L3*

### Galerie le Chariot
A wonderful Inuit art collection awaits souvenir hunters in this gallery on Place Jacques-Cartier. One of the first businesses to preserve buildings in the Old Town, Galerie Le Chariot has treasures to suit all budgets. 🔊 *446 Place Jacques-Cartier • Map L3*

### Camtec Photo
This is the place for all your photography needs. They have their own laboratory on the premises for both 35-mm film and digital equipment and a staff that understands the importance of those once-in-a-lifetime pictures. 🔊 *26 rue Notre-Dame Est • Map K3 • Dis. access*

### Noël Eternel
A store dedicated to the idea of keeping the Christmas spirit alive throughout the year. Stock up on unusual hand-crafted adornments, wrapping paper, stockings, games and dolls. 🔊 *461 rue St-Sulpice • Map K3*

### Conseil des Métiers d'Art du Québec
A sensational cooperative featuring Québecois artists working with varied materials. Choose from paintings, prints, jewelry, clothing, toys, cards, glasswork, marionettes and other fabulous gifts. 🔊 *350 rue St-Paul Est • Map L3*

### Le Cartet Boutique Alimentaire
Drop in at this culinary emporium for the most delicious treats and foodstuffs. With goodies from around the planet, this tempting shop will set your senses ablaze. 🔊 *106 rue McGill • Map J3*

### Renata Morales
A boutique for women who are looking for colorful and original clothing designs. 🔊 *209 rue St-Paul Ouest • Map K3*

### Galerie Clarence Gagnon
Conveniently located across from Marché Bonsecours, this well-stocked gallery not only sells fine artworks but also provides evaluation, consultation, restoration, authentication and framing services. 🔊 *301 rue St-Paul Est • Map L3*

*Following pages:* **Basilique Notre-Dame at night**

59

Left **Aszú** Right **Le Vieux Saint-Gabriel**

# TOP 10 Bars and Cafés

### 1 Aszú
Wine lovers gather at this cozy place that also features one of the most splendid terraces in Vieux-Montréal and a warming fireplace. The menu has been designed to match the many international wines and Champagnes available by the glass. ✆ *212 rue Notre Dame Ouest • Map K3*

### 2 La Cage aux Sports
A boisterous crowd, yet friendly and welcoming, fills this tavern-like sports bar which includes numerous big-screen TVs, a great choice of beers and sports memorabilia on the walls. ✆ *395 rue Le Moyne • Map J3*

### 3 Metropolis
Some of the biggest names and hottest acts play at this popular venue. ✆ *59 rue Ste-Catherine Est • Map L2*

### 4 Toqué!
This is Montréal's most written about restaurant, which offers a ground-breaking, highly original menu. Reservations are a must. ✆ *900 Place Jean-Paul Riopelle • Map D4*

### 5 Le Vieux Saint-Gabriel
One of the oldest inns in North America (1754) is now a bar/restaurant set in a romantic location with inspired French architecture. An extensive wine selection is available. ✆ *426 rue St-Gabriel • Map K3*

### 6 Auberge Pierre du Calvet
A celebrated inn where Benjamin Franklin met with the Sons of Liberty in 1775. It has a cozy lounge with fireplace and an interior atrium garden where breakfast is served *(see p58)*.

### 7 Galiano's
Locals flock to this lively bar in the center of Vieux-Montréal, where atmosphere reigns and draft beer is on tap. Moderately priced wines too. There's also an excellent *table d'hôte* Italian menu. ✆ *410 rue St-Vincent • Map L3*

### 8 Chez Brandy
The bar attached to the popular Keg Steak House attracts a coterie of regulars spanning a wide range of occupations, nationalities and storytelling talents. ✆ *25 rue St-Paul Est • Map L3*

### 9 Stash Café
A favorite actors' hangout near the Centaur Theatre *(see p40)*, this Polish café/restaurant has a superb kitchen serving hearty *borscht* soup, great sausages and authentic apple strudel. ✆ *200 rue St-Paul Ouest • Map K3*

### 10 Santos
For a relaxed evening in Vieux-Montréal, head to laid-back Santos, where you can sample a wide range of drinks and unusual *tapas*-style foods. There is live jazz during the week, and DJs play eclectic sets on weekends. ✆ *191 rue St-Paul Est • Map L3*

*Recommend your favorite bar on traveldk.com*

**Price Categories**

| | |
|---|---|
| For a three-course meal for one with a glass of house wine, and all unavoidable extra charges including tax. | **$** under $20 |
| | **$$** $20–$40 |
| | **$$$** $40–$55 |
| | **$$$$** $55–$80 |
| | **$$$$$** over $80 |

Above **Kashmir**

# 🔟 Restaurants

### Le Petit Moulinsart
If you're a fan of *Tintin* comic books then you will appreciate the kitsch decor of this restaurant. Over 150 beers are available and a Belgian menu – try the mussels. ◎ *139 rue St-Paul Ouest • Map K3 • (514) 843-7432 • $$*

### Nuances
Nouvelle cuisine in a dream-like setting attracts gamblers and tourists alike to this gourmet restaurant. Nuances is regularly awarded the *Mobil Travel Guide's* 5-star rating. Smart dress code. ◎ *1 ave du Casino, Ile Notre-Dame • Map E6 • (514) 392-2708 • Dis. access • $$$$$*

### Restaurant Chez L'Epicier
A fabulous grocery store, sit-down restaurant and take-out service under one roof. Inventive soups, salads and locally produced cheeses, meats and herbs. ◎ *311 rue St-Paul Est • Map L3 • (514) 878-2232 • Dis. access • $$$$*

### Boris Bistro
A sensational mix here – in the lush garden try French fries cooked in duck fat and divine poached salmon. ◎ *465 rue McGill • Map J3 • (514) 848-9575 • $$$*

### Club Chasse et Pêche
This high-end restaurant housed in a low, red-brick building serves a robust mix of fresh seafood and hearty meat dishes. ◎ *423 rue St-Claude • Map L3 • (514) 861-1112 • $$*

### Holder
This elegant Holder brothers restaurant-brasserie exudes flair and good taste. ◎ *407 rue McGill • Map J3 • (514) 849-0333 • $$$*

### Restaurant Hélène de Champlain
Guests will be won over at this Ile Ste-Hélène place, with plush surroundings, comfortable sofas, fireplaces and French cuisine. ◎ *200 Tour de l'Isle, Ile Ste-Hélène • Map F5 • (514) 395-2424 • Dis. access • $$$$*

### Restaurant Solmar
A Portuguese mainstay renowned for its lobster, *filet mignon* and squid. ◎ *111 rue St-Paul Est • Map L3 • (514) 861-4562 • $$$*

### Gibby's
One of Canada's finest eateries, with a courtyard garden and a menu highlighted by oysters and steak. ◎ *298 place d'Youville • Map K3 • (514) 282-1837 • $$$$*

### Kashmir
Haute cuisine from northern India. Their three-course meal specialties include chicken vindaloo and butter chicken, among many others. ◎ *138 rue St-Paul Est • Map L3 • (514) 861-6640 • $$*

Left **Musée d'Art Contemporain de Montréal** Right **Chinatown**

# Downtown and Quartier Latin

THE TWO MOST ANIMATED AND COLORFUL AREAS *of central Montréal offer a cornucopia of delights for visitors and residents alike. Though tiny by many mega-city standards, these quartiers (districts) are intriguing components of Montréal's urban landscape, bustling with activity around the clock as its most hip neighborhoods. They are home to many artists, designers, musicians, writers and academics, as well as students from both Concordia and McGill universities, all of whom are attracted by the eclectic mélange of historic sights, wonderful museums, colorful bars, multi-ethnic restaurants and enclaves, gay and lesbian venues and entrepreneurial businesses. Day-trippers, sightseers and suburban residents contribute equally to this vigorous canvas. No visit to Montréal would be complete without spending at least a couple of days exploring these two magnetic areas of the city.*

## 🔟 Sights

| | | | |
|---|---|---|---|
| **1** | Musée des Beaux-Arts | **6** | Musée Redpath |
| **2** | McCord Museum of Canadian History | **7** | Canadian Centre for Architecture |
| **3** | McGill University | **8** | Chinatown |
| **4** | Cathédrale Marie-Reine-du-Monde | **9** | Chapelle Notre-Dame-de-Lourdes |
| **5** | Musée d'Art Contemporain de Montréal | **10** | Gay Village |

Downtown

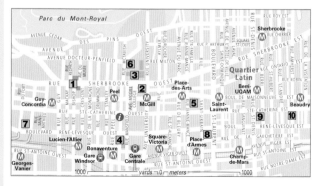

*Sign up for DK's email newsletter on traveldk.com*

### Musée des Beaux-Arts
One of the oldest Canadian bastions of visual and decorative arts. The museum houses vast permanent collections and visiting exhibitions heralding the accomplishments of contemporary artists, as well as creative works by masters from other eras (see pp20–21).

### McCord Museum of Canadian History
The single most important First Nations (native Canadian) collection of artifacts in Québec is on permanent display at the McCord Museum, and includes the most extensive library of costumes and textiles in Canada. Perhaps the most thrilling attraction is the Notman Photographic Archives, which record life in Montréal, Québec and Canada from 1840 to 1935. Over one million pictures are preserved, identified and housed in over 200 albums, which experts around the world use for research purposes. ✎ 690 rue Sherbrooke Ouest • Map J1 • (514) 398 7100 • Open 10am–6pm Tue–Fri, 10am–5pm Sat–Sun • Adm • www.mccord-museum.qc.ca

Inuit slippers, McCord Museum

### McGill University
A remarkable campus spreads itself over 80 lush acres of the Downtown district. The land was a bequest from Scottish fur-trader James McGill in 1821 and was chartered by King George IV. Fine examples of Victorian architecture mix easily with the contemporary bustle of student life, making the 80 buildings on campus a testament to McGill's personal dream and a city's passion for education – McGill's School of Medicine has one of the finest reputations in the world. With over 30,000 students active around the city center, McGill is considered an integral contributor to the dynamics of this handsome neighborhood. ✎ 805 rue Sherbrooke Ouest • Map J1

### Cathédrale Marie-Reine-du-Monde
Reminiscent of Saint Peter's Basilica in Rome, the cathedral was built in the 19th century to service the local Catholic community. It continues to attract visitors and residents, not least because of outstanding architectural features such as the neo-Baroque copper and gold baldachin above the altarpiece. This grand lady remains firmly at the heart of Montréal's Downtown activity. ✎ 1085 rue de la Cathédrale • Map H2 • Open 6:30am–7:30pm Mon–Fri; 7:30am–8:30pm Sat; 8:30am–7:30pm Sun • Free

Altar, Cathédrale Marie-Reine-du-Monde

The best time to absorb the local ambiance of this neighborhood is during the week without the weekend visitors.

## The Heart of French Nationalism

The Quartier Latin neighborhood, thought by some to be the center of French nationalism in Québec, remains a bastion of independent thinkers, artists, writers, academics and students who contribute to a lively backdrop for the ongoing intellectual and political debate concerning the French role in Canada.

### Musée d'Art Contemporain de Montréal

The only museum of art in Canada dedicated solely to contemporary art, this high-profile institution has an innovative program of exhibitions highlighting the work of artists from Canada and the international circuit. ◎ *185 rue Ste-Catherine Ouest • Map K1 • (514) 847 6226 • Open 11am–6pm Tue–Sun (until 9pm Wed) • Dis. access • Adm • www.macm.org*

### Musée Redpath

One of the oldest museums in Canada was opened in 1882 to house the collections of Sir William Dawson, a noted Canadian natural scientist. Part of McGill's Faculty of Science, it now displays biological, geological and cultural artifacts. The building is also notable – commissioned in 1880, it is steeped in Victorian Classicism married together with Greek Revival architecture. ◎ *859 rue Sherbrooke Ouest • Map C3 • Open 9am–5pm Mon–Fri, 1–5pm Sun • Free • www.mcgill.ca/redpath*

### Canadian Centre for Architecture

This award-winning center opened in 1979 to build public awareness about architecture within society; it promotes scholarly research in the field and stimulates innovation in design practice. Its collections, housed in two buildings, one of which is the restored 1874 Shaughnessy House, include models, drawings and photographs of some of the world's most important buildings. Do not miss the gardens across the street. ◎ *1920 rue Baile • Map B4 • (514) 939 7026 • Open 11am–6pm Wed–Sun (until 9pm Thu) • Dis. access • Adm (except Thu) • www.cca.qc.ca*

### Chinatown

Canada's distinguished transcontinental railway system owes a great debt to the many Chinese laborers who made it a reality. After 1880, when the railway was finished, Chinese workers decided to settle in Montréal and gathered together in this enclave to protect themselves against local discrimination. Today the area is also home to many other Southeast Asian communities. A stroll through the lantern-lit streets around boulevard Saint-Laurent and rue de la Gauchetière will impress visitors with bargain boutiques, inexpensive ethnic eateries and cultural hodge-podge. ◎ *Map L2*

Musée Redpath façade

### 9 Chapelle Notre-Dame-de-Lourdes

This richly decorated chapel is the greatest achievement of artist Napoleon Bourassa, grandson of Louis-Joseph Papineau, the father of Québec nationalism. Bourassa studied in Paris, Rome and Venice, returning to Montréal with the desire to create fine art as an expression of patriotism and faith. The chapel was erected in 1876 for the Sulpician Order.
◆ 430 rue Ste-Catherine Est • Map L1 • Open 7am–6:30pm daily • Free

Gay Village

### 10 Gay Village

Montréal is a gay-friendly city, so much so that one of the most festive parades each year belongs to this expanding community. Located between rue St-Hubert and avenue Papineau, the Village is alive with activity around the clock. Restored homes mix with contemporary condominiums to create a diverse and exciting area attracting visitors from around the globe – Montréal was also the site of the first ever World Outgames in 2006. ◆ Map M1

## A Morning Walk through Chinatown and Quartier-Latin

🕐 Start at St Patrick's Basilica *(corner of rue St-Alexandre and blvd René-Lévesque Ouest)* to explore the nave of this wonderful church, then take rue de la Gauchetière east across to ave Viger. Notice the beautiful Chinese lantern streetlights while you continue on to the bargain shops, *dim sum* restaurants, fresh produce markets and herbal stores. Go down St-Urbain to the Holiday Inn Select Montréal Centre-Ville *(99 ave Viger Ouest • Map K2)* to the second-floor Jardins Chinois – a superb stop for a quiet drink.

Exit the hotel, turn right back on to rue de la Gauchetière, turn right again, then continue to boulevard St-Laurent, the heart of **Chinatown** and the main street dividing Montréal into east and west. Make your way to rue St-Denis and turn left. You will now have an opportunity to savor the effervescence of the Quartier-Latin and succumb to the boutiques, restaurants, bistros and cafés. Enter the stunning Saint-Sulpice Library *(1700 rue St-Denis • Map L2)* to see the stained-glass ceilings. Continue north to Carré St-Louis, the center of the quarter with a distinctly French ambiance. Beautiful *belle époque* homes abound in this area, especially on avenue Laval.

Continue the French theme for lunch on the terrace of **Café Cherrier** *(see p73)*.

Left **Underground City** Right **Les Halles de la Gare**

# 🔟 Shopping in Underground City

### 1 Place Bonaventure
More than 135 shops that sell merchandise from all over the world, plus restaurants, cinemas, banks, a post office and a supermarket can be found at this vast complex. ✆ *900 rue de la Gauchetière Ouest • Map J2 • Dis. access*

### 2 Les Halles de la Gare
This innovative structure has evolved into a large concourse for affordable eateries and fashion boutiques, as well as florists, serving downtown workers and train commuters. ✆ *895 rue de la Gauchetière Ouest • Map J2 • Dis. access*

### 3 Centre Eaton
A light-filled glass cavern forms the entrance to this multi-layered shopping mall. Inside are restaurants, shops and six cinemas. ✆ *Rue Ste-Catherine Ouest at ave McGill College • Map J1 • Dis. access*

### 4 Place Montréal Trust
Place Montréal Trust boasts the highest spouting water fountain in North America at 30 m (100 ft) and exclusive fashion outlets. ✆ *Rue Ste-Catherine Ouest at ave McGill College • Map J1 • Dis. access*

### 5 Les Promenades de la Cathédrale
A remarkable underground shopping concourse of 75 stores, built beneath the Christ Church Cathedral (1859). ✆ *625 rue Ste-Catherine Ouest • Map J1 • Dis. access*

### 6 Les Cours Mont-Royal
At the western end of the central shopping network, this mall has the distinction of being set in the 1920s Mont-Royal Hotel, with elegant shops above and below ground. ✆ *1455 rue Peel • Map H1*

### 7 Place Ville-Marie
Place Ville Marie attracts consumers in large numbers, particularly with the Marché Movenpick providing a variety of delicious European food. ✆ *Ave McGill College at rue Cathcart • Map J1 • Dis. access*

### 8 Complexe Desjardins
Across from the Place des Arts, this predominantly French mall is connected to Complex Guy-Favreau and Chinatown via underground tunnels. ✆ *Rue Ste-Catherine Ouest at rue Jeanne-Mance • Map K1 • Dis. access*

### 9 La Baie
Also known as Hudson's Bay Company and The Bay in the rest of the country, this is a historic Canadian department store. All the standard fare, from fashion to household goods. ✆ *585 rue Ste-Catherine Ouest • Map J1 • Dis. access*

### 10 Faubourg Sainte-Catherine
In the heart of Shaughnessy Village this colorful glass mall is known for its fresh market fare and inexpensive eateries. ✆ *1616 rue Ste-Catherine Ouest • Map G1*

With 31 km of passages linking malls, office towers and Métro stations, Montréal's underground city is the largest in the world.

Left **Bar Jello** Right **Drinking in a Downtown bar**

# TOP 10 Bars and Nightclubs

### Club Stéréo
One of the most powerful audio systems in any club in North America continues to pack this after-hours dance floor. A cross section of music styles attracts party animals. ◎ *858 rue Ste-Catherine Est • Map M1 • Dis. access*

### Bar Jello
A sensational martini bar with lava lamps and a rotation of live music acts covering jazz, blues, soul, reggae and world music to set your feet in motion on the dance floor. ◎ *151 rue Ontario Est • Map L1 • Dis. access*

### Club Campus
The best gay strip club in North America receives unanimously positive coverage for the good-looking staff and upbeat atmosphere. ◎ *1111 rue Ste-Catherine Est • Map M1 • Dis. access*

### Pub l'Ile Noir
An authentic Scottish pub with wood decor and an excellent selection of single malt scotches and imported draught beer. The cosy ambiance makes up for the high prices. ◎ *342 rue Ontario Est • Map L1*

### Sky Complex
This amazingly large gay complex features a pub, a dance club and a cabaret to entertain the large and growing gay and lesbian population on the east side of downtown. ◎ *1474 rue Ste-Catherine Est • Map M1 • Dis. access*

### Sofa Bar
A stylish lounge, decorated with candles and sofas and stocking delicious port and a range of cigars. ◎ *451 rue Rachel Est • Map E2*

### Pub Quartier-Latin
One of the most comfortable bars in town. There's a lovely terrace, a cosy bar and a fabulous array of imported and domestic beer. ◎ *318 rue Ontario Est • Map L1 • Dis. access*

### Les Trois Brasseurs
A lively location that opens onto rue St-Denis on two sides with a superb terrace overlooking the flow of festivities. Serves wholesome cuisine and home-brewed beer. ◎ *1660 rue St-Denis • Map E2*

### Pub Sainte-Elisabeth
An Irish pub with a welcoming ambiance, extensive selection of bottled and draught beers, abundant whiskies, ports, wines and buffet food. It also features a secluded garden, fireplace, terrace and friendly bartenders. ◎ *1412 rue Ste-Elisabeth • Map L2*

### Bar Saint-Sulpice
A well known bar popular with university students as the perfect place to party. Contemporary music inside and a massive outdoor garden make for an ideal night out. ◎ *1680 rue St-Denis • Map L1*

*Following pages:* **Downtown skyline at night**

Left **Le Latini** Right **Le Café des Beaux-Arts**

# 🔟 Downtown Restaurants

### 1 Sakura Gardens
A favorite for authentic Japanese food since 1973. The *sushi* and *sashimi* are tasty, but the diverse grilled fish selections and bento boxes are also worth a try. ⊛ *2170 rue de la Montagne • Map C3 • (514) 288-9122 • Dis. access • $$$*

### 2 Le Latini
The Italian restaurant of choice for the glitterati, who enjoy its lively atmosphere, large wine list and sensational chefs. Don't miss *tiramisù* for dessert. ⊛ *1130 rue Jeanne-Mance • Map K2 • (514) 861-3166 • Dis. access • $$$$*

### 3 Le Café des Beaux-Arts
French bistro cuisine awaits you inside the luxurious confines of the Musée des Beaux-Arts *(see pp20–21)*. Delicious, creative dishes and a well-stocked wine list. ⊛ *1384 rue Sherbrooke Ouest • Map C3 • (514) 843-3233 • Dis. access • $$$*

### 4 Tour de Ville
Visually stunning, at the top of Hotel Delta Centre-Ville. The buffet, whose theme changes periodically, will surprise you with its originality. ⊛ *777 rue University • Map J2 • (514) 879-4777 • Dis. access • $$$*

### 5 Alpenhaus
The best *wienerschnitzel*, fondue, goulash and strudel in the city. The Heidi Room can be booked for group celebrations. ⊛ *1279 rue St-Marc • Map B3 • (514) 935-2285 • $$$*

### 6 Eggspectations
A breakfast chain serving American-style fare as well as eggs Benedict and smoked salmon. ⊛ *1313 blvd de Maisonneuve Ouest • Map H1 • (514) 842-3447 • $*

### 7 Le Beaver Club
This famous room inside the Queen Elizabeth Hotel is the best place in Montréal for clam chowder, roast beef and martinis. No jeans or T-shirts. ⊛ *900 blvd René-Lévesque Ouest • Map H2 • (514) 861-3511 • Dis. access • $$$$$*

### 8 Newtown
An entertainment complex owned by racing driver Jacques Villeneuve. ⊛ *1476 rue Crescent • Map G1 • (514) 284-6555 • $$$$$*

### 9 Café Ferreira
Fabulous seafood risotto, and sardines grilled in the finest Portuguese tradition. ⊛ *1446 rue Peel • Map H1 • (514) 848-0988 • $$$$*

### 10 Julien
An authentic Parisian bistro. Try the Noilly Prat vermouth chicken with mushrooms and the *marquise fondante au chocolat* (chocolate-lover's ring). ⊛ *1191 ave Union • Map J2 • (514) 871-1581 • $$$*

**Price Categories**

For a three-course meal for one with a glass of house wine, and all unavoidable extra charges including tax.

| | |
|---|---|
| **$** | under $20 |
| **$$** | $20–$40 |
| **$$$** | $40–$55 |
| **$$$$** | $55–$80 |
| **$$$$$** | over $80 |

Above **Café Cherrier**

# 🔟 Quartier Latin Restaurants

### 1 La Paryse
Often considered the best burgers in Canada, variants include double patties, cream cheese, bacon and soy substitutes. A young, arty ambiance. ◈ *302 rue Ontario Est • Map L1 • (514) 842-2040 • Dis. access • $$*

### 2 Restaurant Laloux
Seasonal ingredients are lavishly presented on an ever-changing menu devised by chef Marc-André Jetté. The dessert menu is equally satisfying. ◈ *250 ave des Pins Est • Map D3 • (514) 287-9127 • Dis. access • $$$*

### 3 Restaurant Nouveau Delhi
The king of Montréal's Indian eateries serves creative and sumptuous cuisine in an atmosphere of white linen, silverware and impeccable service. ◈ *3434 rue St-Denis • Map E3 • (514) 845-7977 • Dis. access • $$*

### 4 Café Cherrier
This bustling French bistro has one of the best terraces in Montréal which makes its weekend brunches quite a social event. ◈ *3635 rue St-Denis • Map E3 • (514) 843-4308 • Dis. access • $$*

### 5 Nonya
A Malaysian newcomer that is becoming a local favorite with sensational *Lumpia Goreng* (egg rolls) and *Sate Ayan* (grilled chicken in peanut sauce). ◈ *151 Bernard Ouest • Map C1 • (514) 875-9998 • Dis. access • $$*

### 6 La Couscoussiere
A Moroccan/Tunisian restaurant that serves authentic fare in exotic surroundings. ◈ *1460 rue Amherst • Map M1 • (514) 842-6667 • Dis. access • $*

### 7 Les Deux Charentes
Roast salmon with pine nuts heads the list of French dishes here, along with duck with maple syrup. ◈ *815 blvd de Maisonneuve Est • Map M1 • (514) 523-1132 • $$$*

### 8 O'Thym
This chic BYO (bring your own wine) bistro features dishes based on local ingredients, including venison and salmon. ◈ *1112 blvd de Maisonneuve Est (cnr Amherst) • Map M1 • (514) 525-3443 • $$*

### 9 Le Grille Pain
This tiny breakfast specialty house is jammed daily because of its delicious French toast and Belgian waffles. ◈ *950 rue Roy Est • Map E2 • (514) 527-8500 • $*

### 🔟 Café Saigon
Popular with the university crowd, this Asian café is famous for its shrimp soup and spring rolls. ◈ *1280 rue St-André • Map M1 • (514) 849-0429 • Dis. access • $*

Left **Rue St-Denis** Right **Boulevard St-Laurent**

# Mont-Royal to Hochelaga-Maisonneuve

THIS GENEROUS SWATH OF MONTRÉAL *includes the most dominant green space and some of the finest attractions of the entire city. The fertile, rolling expanse that makes up Parc du Mont-Royal spreads gracefully into the bustle below – captivating areas such as Little Italy, Rosemont and Mercier, with a rich ethnic mix flavoring the street life. Here you'll find shops, markets and restaurants offering every imaginable temptation. For those favoring the outdoor life, the mountain provides an inviting backdrop for a wide range of activities. As a fitting monument to this dynamic core of Montréal, the Parc Olympique beckons guests east to the Quartier Hochelaga-Maisonneuve. The Stade Olympique, the Jardin Botanique and the Biodôme and Insectarium provide visitors, young and old, with an array of entertainment options.*

## 🔟 Sights

| | |
|---|---|
| **1** Parc du Mont-Royal | **6** Avenue du Mont-Royal |
| **2** Parc Olympique | **7** Avenue du Parc |
| **3** Rue Saint-Denis | **8** Outremont |
| **4** Boulevard Saint-Laurent | **9** Little Italy |
| **5** Le Plateau Mont-Royal | **10** Marché Jean-Talon |

**Parc du Mont-Royal**

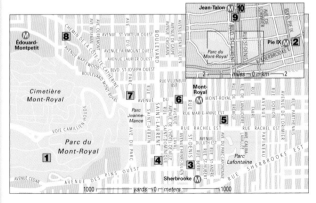

**Biodôme, Parc Olympique**

### Parc du Mont-Royal

Mont Royal, after which Montréal is named, defines the city's personality with its year-round outdoor attractions, multi-ethnic cemetery and lush, rolling breadth overlooking the St Lawrence River. Parc du Mont-Royal has attained the distinction of being the only place in Québec to receive both historic and natural heritage status from the government, which means that it is protected forever as a green space for all to enjoy *(see pp8–11)*.

### Parc Olympique

This astonishing attraction offers exhilarating activities for all age groups. From the dizzying heights of the world's highest leaning tower, the Tour de Montréal atop the Stade Olympique; through the jungle environment of the Biodôme, home to numerous indigenous wild plants and animals; and to the 200 beautiful acres of the Jardin Botanique – you can easily spend a full day or two exploring this area *(see pp14–17)*.

### Rue Saint-Denis

Architectural treasures, street poets, clothing stores and a plethora of restaurants and cafés are the main attractions on this street. From Old Montréal's Carré Viger north to Carré Saint-Louis, the Victorian architecture seems to blend effortlessly with the designer stores, hip-hop music culture and the buzzing youthful vitality that is the essence of this area. 🔊 *Map E2*

### Boulevard Saint-Laurent

East meets west at this long boulevard, commonly referred to as "the Main". Beginning at the waterfront, it designates the symbolic dividing line between the Anglophone west side and the Francophone east side of the city, although contemporary Montréal finds the division all but vanished these days. Here you'll find designer boutiques, chic cafés and *sushi* bars, gourmet restaurants and up-to-the-minute nightclubs sometimes stacked two and three high, underlining the street's international party reputation. As for shopping, you can buy almost anything you desire here, from cheap clothing to food, antiquarian books, high-tech equipment, diamonds, old newspapers, woodcarvings and other crafts, kitchenware – even gravestones. 🔊 *Map D2*

### Maison de la Culture

Montréal has one of the most prized cultural networks in the world, evident in a system of venues called Maison de la Culture (house of culture) where music, art and symposia are offered to the public for free or at minimal cost. The best example is the Chapelle Historique du Bon-Pasteur at 100 rue Sherbrooke Est, which has become a concert hall.

### Le Plateau Mont-Royal

Plateau Mont-Royal begins to blossom at rue Sherbrooke and boulevard Saint-Laurent and spreads northward to avenue Laurier and east to Parc Lafontaine. This architecturally rich neighborhood was made up of separate villages before being absorbed by the City of Montréal. Ornate duplexes abound on tree-lined streets, where you can see exterior staircases, wrought-iron banisters and fine woodwork. The area shines day or night with colorful clubs, shops, markets and restaurants. ✎ Map E2

Le Plateau Mont-Royal

### Avenue du Mont-Royal

This street has vitality and panache, reflected in its bevy of eclectic eateries, curiosity shops and cafés but mostly in the laid-back attitude of its residents. Bargain shops nestle beside haute couture boutiques, while markets sell everything from hip fashion to ethnic cuisine. ✎ Map D2

Tam-Tam Festival, Avenue du Parc

### Avenue du Parc

Starting at rue Sherbrooke heading north, this riotous thoroughfare slices through the principal neighborhoods of the city: McGill Ghetto, Parc Mont-Royal, Le Plateau Mont-Royal, Mile End and Park Extension. It is possible to spend a whole day on this one street alone, starting with breakfast at Chez Cora's, enjoying the mountain's Tam-Tam drum festival (Sundays only), sampling an authentic Greek, Lebanese or Italian lunch, shopping for bargains or custom-made leather coats in the afternoon, then stopping for a swim at the YMCA, and finally enjoying a drink while listening to live African music. ✎ Map D2
• Cora's: 3465 ave du Parc • YMCA: 5550 ave du Parc

### Outremont

Founded in 1695, this area, meaning "beyond the mountain", is the predominantly French-speaking wealthy residential quarter. It features some of the most luxurious mansions in the city, and the main thoroughfares of avenue Laurier and rue Bernard west of avenue du Parc are peppered with expensive fashion boutiques, exclusive hair salons, and hip eateries serving a clientele more akin to Paris than North America. Don't miss one of the country's finest *fromageries* (cheese-makers), Fromagerie Yannick or the rich cakes at Pâtisserie de Gascogne. The area is one of the few areas in the city where you can actually get lost due to the meandering streets, so keep a mental note of your route. 🖎 *Map C1 • Fromagerie Yannick: 1218 rue Bernard • Pâtisserie de Gascogne: 237 ave Laurier*

### 9 Little Italy

Italian Canadians provide another spice of life to Montréal's ethnic blend and make up the largest immigrant community, tracing their presence in the city back to the early 19th century. Boulevard Saint-Laurent provides the Italian version of café society in a stream of cafés and restaurants, but Little Italy proper is defined by the borders of rue Jean-Talon, rue Saint-Zotique, rue Marconi and avenue Drolet. Here you can indulge in the most authentic pasta, pizza and strong *espresso* coffee. 🖎 *Métro Jean-Talon*

### 10 Marché Jean-Talon

A walk through the alluring Marché Jean-Talon tempts the senses with a profusion of fresh market fare, imported Italian gourmet luxuries and homemade marvels from traditional local kitchens. Fresh produce is brought to market by dozens of farmers from outlying regions, together with discerning local importers. Also inside the market area is the Marché des Saveurs du Québec, which departs from the Italian theme and presents a line up of specialties from Québec Province. 🖎 *Métro Jean-Talon*

## A Day's Walk Around Mont-Royal

🕐 Take the No. 11 bus from Mont-Royal Métro station up **avenue du Mont-Royal** and you will be able to see the **Parc Olympique** *(see pp14–17)* to the east. Disembark at **Lac aux Castors** *(see p9)* and walk around the lakeside trail to see resident ducks and geese. Follow the trail, veering to your left, to chemin Olmsted, which leads you past sculptures of the International Sculpture Symposium. Continue to **Maison Smith** *(see pp14–17)*, and take in the wonderful exhibit presented by Les amis de la montagne (Friends of the Mountain).

Return to chemin Olmsted and follow the trail left to the commemorative Olmsted plaque embedded in rock and then on to the main chalet and **Kondiaronk Lookout** *(see p8)*. This is the most outstanding viewpoint of the city. Return to the path behind the chalet, turn right and a little further on climb the path on your left to the foot of **La Croix** *(see p8)*, the most recognized symbol of Montréal.

Return to Maison Smith to take the bus back to Mont-Royal Métro station then continue east along avenue du Mont-Royal on foot. This street buzzes with commotion and you can choose from a feast of tantalizing cafés for lunch.

### Afternoon

You can either spend the afternoon enjoying some of the best shopping in the area on ave Duluth, or relax, weather permitting, in the lovely **Parc Lafontaine** *(see p36)*.

Around Montréal – Mont-Royal to Hochelaga-Maisonneuve

Left **Barraca Rhumerie et Tapas** Right **Aux Deux Maries**

# ⬛ Bars and Cafés

### Moe's Deli & Bar
A fabulous deli-chain, this is the best spot to stock up for a picnic in nearby Parc Olympique. It's also a sports bar attracting a crowd of regulars for hockey games. ◈ *3950 rue Sherbrooke Est • Map E3*

### Barraca Rhumerie et Tapas
A tightly packed spot popular with young people who have a penchant for rum. Dozens of brands from 11 countries are served alongside delicious *tapas*. ◈ *1134 ave du Mont-Royal Est • Map E2*

### Bílý Kůň
This hip micro-brewery pub serves up creamy house-brewed beer as well as many other quality drinks. ◈ *354 ave du Mont-Royal Est • Map E2*

### Quai des Brumes
A cozy bar favored by intellectuals and musicians. Right in the heart of Le Plateau Mont-Royal *(see 76)*, Quai des Brumes also offers live music for a minimal cover charge, and often for free. ◈ *4481 rue St-Denis • Map E2 • Dis. access*

### Café Rico
Stéphane Tamar Kordahi opened Café Rico as a politically conscious place serving fair-trade coffee. It has succeeded in creating a relaxed, musical ambiance with the constant and welcoming aroma of roasting beans. ◈ *969 rue Rachel Est • Map E2*

### Aux Deux Maries
One of the best coffee houses on this competitive stretch of rue Saint-Denis. The proprietors roast their own beans which come directly from Costa Rica, Kenya, Ethiopia and beyond. Great desserts and atmosphere. ◈ *4329 rue St-Denis • Map E2 • Dis. access*

### Bières & Compagnie
Celtic music, home-brewed beer as well as imports mix well with the multicultural ambiance. ◈ *4350 rue St-Denis • Map E2*

### Vol de Nuit
This stalwart watering hole has the best terrace bar in the city for people-watching – the crowds on the pedestrian walkway present an endless stream of fascinating characters. ◈ *14 rue Prince-Arthur • Map D3*

### El Zaz Bar
A landmark in Montréal's Plateau district, the El Zaz Bar hosts musical acts of all stripes. They also have DJs who are up spinning tunes seven nights a week. ◈ *4297 rue St-Denis • Map E2*

### Else's
This is a favored neighborhood bar for musicians, artists and Bohemian types, and it is a relatively quiet perch in the middle of a bustling quarter. Else's serves a selection of simple foods too. ◈ *156 rue Roy Est • Map E2*

**Price Categories**

| | |
|---|---|
| For a three-course meal for one with a glass of house wine, and all unavoidable extra charges including tax. | **$** under $20 |
| | **$$** $20–$35 |
| | **$$$** $35–$60 |
| | **$$$$** $60–$85 |
| | **$$$$$** over $85 |

Above **Fruits Folies**

#  Restaurants

### Fruits Folies
Sit on the terrace here overlooking rue Saint-Denis and sample delightful crêpes, great sandwiches, strong coffee and excellent service. ✆ *3817 rue St-Denis • Map E2 • (514) 840 9011 • $$*

### Ty-Breiz Crêperie Bretonne
Stepping into this perennial favorite is to taste Bretonne food in many of its traditional forms, from onion soup and frog's legs to the assortment of tantalizing crêpes filled with seafood, sausage or, for dessert, with fruit. ✆ *933 rue Rachel Est • Map E2 • (514) 521 1444 • Dis. access • $$*

### Cocagne Bistro
Stylish presentation of classic French food with Québécois touches makes this a reliable yet interesting dining spot. ✆ *3842 rue St-Denis • Map E2 • (514) 286 0700 • $$$ • www.bistro-cocagne.com*

### Mazurka
*Borscht, wienerschnitzel,* and Polish sausage are just a few reasons why Montréalers flock to this character-filled East European eatery. ✆ *64 rue Prince Arthur Est • Map D3 • (514) 844 3539 • $*

### Patati Patata Friterie Deluxe
Try the delicious breakfasts here or a satisfying dinner of roast beef or fish and chips. Great music and friendly service. ✆ *4177 blvd St-Laurent • Map D2 • (514) 844 0216 • $*

### Savannah
In this Southern-fusion kitchen try jambalaya with jumbo shrimp and great cornbread. ✆ *4448 blvd St-Laurent • Map D2 • (514) 904 0277 • Dis. access • $$$*

### Wilensky's Light Lunch
A Jewish restaurant renowned for its grilled salami and bologna sandwiches. ✆ *34 ave Fairmont Ouest • Map D1 • (514) 271 0247 • Closed Sat–Sun • Dis. access • $*

### Moishe's
This steakhouse has been attracting businessmen for years with their steaks topped with dill pickles. ✆ *3961 blvd St-Laurent • Map D2 • (514) 845 3509 • Dis. access • $$$*

### LeLe da Cuca
Bring your own wine to wash down Brazilian and Mexican specialties. ✆ *70 rue Marie-Anne Est • Map D2 • (514) 849 6649 • $$*

### La Gaudriole
The best gourmet value in town. Try duck foie gras with cranberry compote. ✆ *825 ave Laurier Est • Map E1 • (514) 276 1580 • Dis. access • $$$*

**Note:** Unless otherwise stated, all restaurants accept credit cards and serve vegetarian meals

Left **1000 Islands** Right **Oka ferry, Lac des Deux-Montagnes**

# Excursions from Montréal

O N FRIDAY NIGHTS AND SATURDAY MORNINGS *Montréal's bridges are crowded with residents traveling out of town to enjoy the vast array of activities possible in the countryside surrounding the city. Whether for an afternoon, overnight or long weekend, les Laurentides (the Laurentian mountains) and the villages and hills of Cantons de l'Est (the Eastern Townships) are where Montrealers have traditionally ventured to hike in summer or ski in winter. River traffic through the locks at Sainte-Anne-de-Bellevue also buzzes with yachters and boaters heading west on the Ottawa River or east to Trois-Rivières, Québec City and on to the Atlantic Ocean. Beaches at Parc National d'Oka, Lac Memphrémagog or Lac des Sables are a magnet for sun-lovers in summer.*

## 🔟 Sights

1. Les Laurentides
2. Outaouais
3. Hudson and Rigaud
4. 1000 Islands
5. Deux-Montagnes
6. Lanaudière
7. Montérégie
8. Parc National du Canada de la Mauricie
9. Trois-Rivières
10. Cantons de l'Est

**Les Laurentides town**

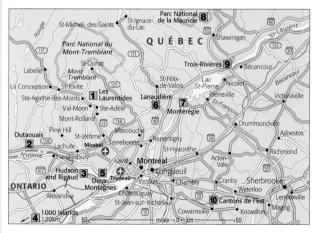

*Sign up for DK's email newsletter on traveldk.com*

**Ski slope, Les Laurentides**

### Les Laurentides
Only an hour from the congestion of Montréal, the stunning Laurentian mountains north of the city provide an astounding list of activities. In summer there are endless opportunities to swim, fish, hunt, raft, horse-ride, play golf, mountain climb, or just relax in the sunny rural setting. Winter brings the chance to ski (downhill or cross-country), go tobogganing or snowboarding, or ice climb (see pp30–31).

### Outaouais
This historic area of the province, west of Montréal, was not settled by white men until the early 19th century, and it remains a largely undeveloped region of lakes and forests. Don't miss Oméga Safari Park, just outside Montebello with its 1,500 acres inhabited by roaming bison, wapitis, black bear, boar and wolves, then continue on to the Parc National de Plaisance along the Ottawa River, to see flocks of Canada geese. In Montebello itself Manoir Louis-Joseph-Papineau is a 19th-century home filled with a collection of antiques and local artifacts. ◈ Map N5 • Oméga Park: 399 rte 323 N • Manoir Louis-Joseph-Papineau: 500 rue Notre-Dame, Montebello; Open May–late Aug: 10am–5pm daily; late Aug–Oct: 10am–5pm Sat–Sun; Adm

### Hudson and Rigaud
A favorite jaunt west from Montréal has traditionally included the communities of Hudson and Rigaud, hugging the mountains along the pastoral Ottawa River. Hudson, with its history of British settlement and fur trading, has a prevalence of historic mansions set on magnificent estates and an abundance of antiques shops, art galleries, and cafés. Its land-scape is a popular destination for equestrians, while its riverside setting draws a keen sailing crowd. In contrast, the village of Rigaud is more of a French area, maintaining its Gallic legacy in elegant churches, convents, guesthouses and family-run farms. ◈ Map N6

### 1000 Islands
These islands are one of Montréal's great escapes and one of Canada's premier tourist areas, accessible either by car or train to Brockville. About two hours west of the border of Ontario and Québec, 1000 Islands actually covers 1,865 islands running the 80-km (50-mile) span from Brockville to Kingston, formed by metamorphic rock at the end of the last Ice Age. St Lawrence Islands National Park is the jewel in the crown. Camp sites are available on 11 of the islands. ◈ Rte No. 401 • Boat trips: St Lawrence Cruise Lines 1-800 267 7868 • www.stlawrencecruiselines.com

For details on outdoor activities in and around Montréal
See pp48–9

**Montérégie**

### Montérégie
**7** To reach this huge region of plains, forests and history, drive across the Pont Champlain following the signs for highway 10 eastward. Then take highway 133 (also called Chemin des Patriotes after the soldiers who fought the British here in 1837) toward Sorel, the fourth oldest city in Canada. Boat trips are possible around the town's many islands. Of major note in the region, which is known for its apple orchards and cider-making, is Fort Chambly in Saint-Denis. This well-preserved 18th-century fortress was built to defend the French from both Dutch and British attack. It is one of many similar forts found in the area.
⊛ Map P5 • www.tourisme-monteregie. qc.ca • Fort Chambly: 2 rue Richelieu, St-Denis • Open Apr–Oct: 10am–5pm Wed–Sun (mid-May–Sep: to 6pm daily) • Adm

### Deux-Montagnes
**5** This community, 30 minutes' drive from Montréal, was first settled by the Sulpician Order during the French Regime, and the fresh produce of this region, including the famous Oka cheese, is a carry-over from the agricultural traditions begun by the priests. Parc National d'Oka offers camping, kayaking, hiking and a sandy beach. ⊛ Map N6

### Lanaudière
**6** From the St Lawrence River Valley rising to the Laurentian lowland plateau, there's a multitude of forests, lakes, rivers and farmland to explore, all within a few hours of Montréal. The Festival de Lanaudière, Canada's most renowned classical music festival, takes place from the end of June to early August, with concerts staged at outdoor venues and heritage churches in Joliette. ⊛ Map P5 • www.tourisme–lanaudiere.qc.ca

### Parc National du Canada de la Mauricie
**8** One of Canada's most spectacular areas of rivers, lakes, mountains and wildlife, La Mauricie National Park is only a two-hour drive from downtown Montréal or Québec City. It is accessible all year round, and is a perennial favorite with campers and outdoor enthusiasts. It is particularly popular with anglers, with trout and pike found in abundance in Lac Wapizagonke. ⊛ Map P4 • Open May–Nov • Dis. access • Adm • www.pc.gc.ca

### Trois-Rivières
**9** Sieur de Laviolette founded this community in 1634, but the beautiful French Regime architecture that once graced the streets was ravaged by a monstrous fire

---

#### Bridges of Montréal
Getting on and off the island city of Montréal can be daunting. Pay due respect to the French "*pont*" (bridge) signage, because once you are on a bridge, you must continue across it before you have the chance to turn around. There are a total of 15 bridges and one tunnel providing access to the city.

---

**Monastère des Ursulines, Trois-Rivières**

that swept through the entire town in 1908. Only remnants of the original wall survive. Today the town is known as one of the main providers of pulp and paper in the world. Dominating the landscape is the Monastère des Ursulines, a lovely church built by Ursuline nuns, surrounded by a public park. Cafés, bistros and restaurants abound on rue des Forges. ◈ *Map Q5*

**Cantons de l'Est**

This natural wonderland is bounded by the Richelieu and St Lawrence rivers and the US states of Vermont, New Hampshire and Maine. The personality of the region owes its profile to the Appalachian Mountains, with top-notch hiking trails at Owl's Head, Mont Sutton, Mont Bromont and Mont Orford. The peaceful villages throughout this vast district, such as Knowlton, are a historic remnant of 19th-century British settlement, their Victorian buildings now home to antiques shops and cafés *(see pp84–5)*. ◈ *Map Q6 • www.tourisme–cantons.qc.ca*

## A Day in Val-David and the P'tit Train du Nord Trail

**Morning**

Begin by taking Route 15, the Laurentian Autoroute, north to Exit 76, then join Route 117 north to the village of **Val-David** *(see p31)*. At the Municipalité de Val-David *(2501 rue de l'Eglise)* you can obtain a map and detailed information about the region.

Walk down rue de l'Eglise to visit the Mille et Un Pots gallery and gift shop *(2435 rue de l'Eglise)*. This exhibition of handmade pottery and works of art is the largest ceramic show in North America, produced by an esteemed collective of over 50 Québécois artists. For a great lunch, backtrack to rue de la Sapinière and turn right to Hotel la Sapinière *(1244 chemin de la Sapinière • 1-800 567 6635 • $$$)*.

**Afternoon**

After lunch, explore the **Piste de la P'tit Train du Nord** *(see p48)*, a green swath of protected trails snaking 200 km (125 miles) through the Laurentides on the old mountain train path. The defunct railroad line is perfect for hiking, cycling and walking in summer and cross-country skiing in winter. If cycling is your preference, Roc 'n' Ride *(2444 rue de l'Eglise)* rents bikes.

Return to Val-David and, if you have the energy, shop for unusual Christmas decorations at Village du Père Noël *(987 rue Morin)*, open all year. Then enjoy a traditional Québécois dinner at **Restaurant au Petit Poucet** *(see p87)*.

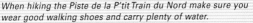

*When hiking the Piste de la P'tit Train du Nord make sure you wear good walking shoes and carry plenty of water.*

Left **Lac Brome, Knowlton** Center **Church, Lac Memphrémagog** Right **Sherbrooke**

# Attractions in Cantons de l'Est

### 1 Zoo de Granby
This zoo is home to over 250 species of animals from exotic countries. ✆ *525 rue St-Hubert, Granby • Map Q6 • Open May–mid-Jun: 10am–5pm daily; mid-Jun–Aug: 10am–7pm daily; Sep–Oct: 10am–5pm Sat & Sun • Adm*

### 2 Parc National du Mont-Orford
Rising majestically beside the Eastern Townships Autoroute, Mont Orford is the central area for outdoor activities in this sprawling preserve, covering over 57 sq km (22 sq miles) around the mountain. ✆ *3221 chemin du Parc, Canton d'Orford • Map Q6*

### 3 Knowlton
Set on the inviting shores of Lac Brome, this 19th-century anglophone village has an idyllic locale, attracting vacationers and weekenders. ✆ *Map Q6*

### 4 Lac Memphrémagog
This immense lake is a draw for boat-lovers. La Traversée Internationale du lac Memphré-magog, an annual international swimming contest, attracts thousands to the nearby town of Magog in summer. ✆ *Map Q6*

### 5 L'Abbaye de Saint-Benoît-du-Lac
Benedictine monks founded this monastery overlooking Lac Memphrémagog in 1913. Their Gregorian chants take place daily at 5pm. ✆ *Saint-Benoît-du-Lac • Map Q6 • Open 5:30am–9pm daily • Free*

### 6 Le Chemin des Vignobles de l'Estrie
Due to its slate soil and climate this area has a highly respected wine-growing tradition visible along the Wine Route (Hwy 202) between Dunham and Stanbridge East. ✆ *Map P6*

### 7 Frelighsburg
A peaceful town at the foot of Mount Pinnacle and near the US border, Frelighsburg's landscape attracts artists and photographers. ✆ *Map P6*

### 8 Lennoxville
Home to Bishop's University and College, this town is one of the few in Québec to remain predominantly English through-out the province's political turmoil. The Uplands Cultural and Heritage Museum unveils its history. ✆ *Map Q6 • Uplands Cultural and Heritage Museum: 9 rue Speid • Open 1–4:30pm Wed–Sun (summer: 10am–4:30pm Tue–Sun), closed Jan • Adm*

### 9 Sherbrooke
The Rivière Saint-François bisects this commercial center of Cantons de l'Est. Despite its history of British settlement, today it is predominantly a French-speaking town. ✆ *Map Q6*

### 10 Parc de la Gorge de Coaticook
This park, set around a 50-m (165-ft) gorge, offers hiking trails, horse riding, as well as skiing in winter *(see p86)*. ✆ *Map Q6*

**Price Categories**

| | |
|---|---|
| For a three-course meal | **$** under $20 |
| for one with a glass of | **$$** $20–$35 |
| house wine, and all | **$$$** $35–$60 |
| unavoidable extra | **$$$$** $60–$85 |
| charges including tax. | **$$$$$** over $85 |

Above **Café Restaurant Adawatea**

# 🔟 Restaurants in Cantons de l'Est

### 1 Café Massawippi
The food and service are the stuff of dreams in this welcoming house. Try mignon of pork with caramelized endive, compote of pear, goat's cheese and tarragon. ◎ *3050 chemin Capelton, North Hatley • Map Q6 • (819) 842 4528 • Closed Sun & Mon (Nov–May) • $$$$*

### 2 Café Restaurant Adawatea
A delightful Victorian home, art gallery, cultural center and tearoom. Sit in the beautiful garden and don't miss the remarkable antiques collection. ◎ *330 chemin de la Rivière, North Hatley • Map Q6 • (819) 842 4440 • $*

### 3 Haut Bois Normand
Experience adventure trails in summer and tubing in winter before sampling traditional Québécois fare. In March, try the *tire sur neige* (maple-syrup taffy on snow). ◎ *26 chemin George-Bonnallie, Eastman • Map Q6 • (450) 297 2659 • Open weekends only • $$*

### 4 Auberge aux Toits Rouges
Local produce features highly at this country inn. One of the highlights is the *filet mignon*. ◎ *72 rue Chesham, Notre-Dame-des-Bois • Off map • (819) 888 2999 • Dis. access • $$$*

### 5 La Tablée du Pont Couvert
Chef-owner André LaPalme provides *"soirées épicurienne"* of five courses and four wine servings. Reservations essential. ◎ *5675 rte 147, R.R.2 Milby • Map Q6 • (819) 837 0014 • $$$*

### 6 Auberge West Brome
Luxurious Auberge West Brome offers Lac Brome duck and other regional specialties, as well as first-class accommodations. ◎ *128 route 139, West Brome • Map Q6 • (450) 266 7552 • Dis. access • $$$*

### 7 L'Oeuf
A gourmet restaurant, *chocolaterie* and auberge specializing in creative dishes, ending with handmade chocolate. ◎ *229 chemin Mystic, Mystic • Map P6 • (450) 248 7529 • Closed Mon & Tue • $$$*

### 8 L'Ancrage
Chef Jeanine Ouellette offers high-end dishes for lunch and dinner on the shores of Lac Memphrémagog. A gourmet six-course meal is also available. ◎ *1200 rue Principale Ouest, Magog • Map Q6 • (819) 843 6521 • Dis. access • $$$$$*

### 9 Aux Berges de l'Aurore
A romantic inn serving venison, caribou, wild boar and maple syrup mousse. ◎ *139 route du Parc, Notre-Dame-des-Bois • Map Q6 • (819) 888 2715 • Closed L, Nov–Apr • $$$*

### 10 Auberge du Joli Vent
Chef Hans Christiner's weekly changing menu features innovative dishes prepared with locally sourced seasonal ingredients, such as Brome Lake duck. ◎ *667 chemin Bondville, Lac-Brome • Map Q6 • (450) 243 4272 • Open Fri & Sat dinner only • $$$*

 **Note:** *Unless otherwise stated, all restaurants accept credit cards and serve vegetarian meals*

Left **Foothills of Mont Sutton** Right **Lac Mégantic**

# 🔟 Natural Sights

### Missisquoi Bay
The traditional home of the Abenaki native people, this lush area in the western corner of Cantons de l'Est was the first refuge for Loyalist settlers crossing into Canada after the American Revolution. ◈ *Map P6*

### The Orchards
The best territory for apples in the province is the Montérégie Region, but Cantons de l'Est also has an abundance of orchards around Dunham, Brigham, Compton and Stanbridge. ◈ *Map Q6*

### Lac Brome
Lac Brome consists of several delightful lakeside communities: Knowlton; Foster; Bondville; Fulford; Iron Hill; East Hill; and West Brome, all of which retain in part a bygone way of life. ◈ *Map Q6*

### Mont Sutton
Since it opened in 1960, Mont Sutton has been a favorite with downhill skiers due to its superior slopes. ◈ *Map Q6*

### Route Saint-Armand
In 1748 the Seigneurie Saint-Armand was given to René Nicholas Levasseur by the King of France and much of this spectacular property can be seen today along the country roads from Vale Perkins on Lake Memphrémagog to the village of Saint-Armand. ◈ *Map Q6*

### Mont Owl's Head
This dramatically positioned family ski destination is set above Lake Memphrémagog and is tied with Mont Orford *(see p84)* as Québec's highest vertical drops. ◈ *Map Q6*

### Lac Massawippi
Sir Anthony Hopkins and Nicole Kidman are among those on the list of regulars at the Manoir Hovey resort here *(see p116)*. Le Festival du Lac Massawippi runs popular music concerts from April until end of June. ◈ *Map Q6*

### Parc de la Gorge de Coaticook
More than 50,000 years ago the Wisconsin Glacier started to melt giving birth to the Coaticook Lake and then this river, which dug a cavernous gorge. It now attracts visitors to the longest pedestrian suspension bridge in the world *(see p84)*. ◈ *Map Q6*

### Parc National du Mont-Mégantic
Stargazing is the rule in this huge natural wonderland as the Astrolab observatory beckons astronomers of every level. ◈ *Rte No. 257*

### Lac Mégantic
Located at the eastern edge of the townships in the Appalachian foothills, this peaceful lake provides outdoor activities including a beach. ◈ *Rte No. 161*

**Price Categories**

For a three-course meal for one with a glass of house wine, and all unavoidable extra charges including tax.

| | |
|---|---|
| **$** | under $20 |
| **$$** | $20–$40 |
| **$$$** | $40–$55 |
| **$$$$** | $55–$80 |
| **$$$$$** | over $80 |

Above **Maple sugar produce**

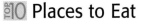

# Places to Eat

**Sucrerie de la Montagne**
Pierre Faucher's famous maple sugar house serves highly traditional Québécois cuisine such as pea soup, *tourtière* (meat pie), wood-fired baked beans, maple-glazed smoked ham, and maple sugar pie. ✆ 300 St Georges Rd, Rigaud • Map N6 • (450) 451 0831 • Dis. access • $$$

**Ferme Apicole Intermiel**
This farm offers wonderful picnic sites with an abundance of apiary products to taste afterwards, such as honey mead and honey cookies. ✆ 10291 rang de la Fresnière, Mirabel • Map N5 • (450) 258 2713 • Closed D • Dis. access • $

**Cap Saint-Jacques Maison de la Ferme Ecologique**
Visit the organic farm, tour the stables then relax on the terrace enjoying a burger, pasta, soups and salads. A store sells organic produce. ✆ 183 chemin du Cap-Saint-Jacques, Pierrefonds • Map N6 • (514) 280 6743 • Closed D • Dis. access • $$

**Perkins Bakery**
Perkins serves homemade bread, muffins, cakes and sweets at its take-out counter, or you can enjoy soups and sandwiches either inside or on the terrace. ✆ 280 Owl's Head Rd, Mansonville • Map Q6 • (450) 292 3160 • Dis. access • $

**Restaurant Les Artistes**
This bistro serves excellent *boeuf Bourguignon* and *médaillon de cerf aux Calvados* (venison with apple brandy). ✆ 116 rue des Remparts, Mont-Tremblant • Map N5 • (819) 681 4606 • Dis. access • $$$

**Willow Place Inn**
Surrounded by water and rolling hills, this relaxing inn serves fish and chips in the pub area, or you can opt for the more formal dining room. ✆ 208 Main Rd, Hudson • Map N6 • (450) 458 7006 • Dis. access • $$$$

**Restaurant au Petit Poucet**
Chef Réjean Campeau produces delectable maple-smoked ham, pig's knuckles, and sugar pie. ✆ 1030 rte 117, Val David • Map N5 • (819) 322 2246 • Dis. access • $$$

**Recto Verso**
Five-star Belgian cuisine. Try rabbit in Liège syrup with two kinds of Belgian beer. ✆ 814 chemin Pierre-Péladeau, Ste-Adèle • Map N5 • (450) 229 9555 • Dis. access • $$$

**Le Bistro à Champlain**
Stellar French cuisine and one of the best wine lists. ✆ 75 chemin Masson, Ste-Marguerite-du-lac-Masson • Map N5 • (450) 228 4988 • Closed L, Mon–Tue • Dis. access • $$$$

**Au Tournant de la Rivière**
Chef Jacques Robert satisfies his passion for wild mushroom hunting by blending them into gastronomic inventions such as veal with tarragon and mushrooms. ✆ 5070 rue Salaberry, Carignan • (450) 658 7372 • Closed L, Mon–Wed • Dis. access • $$$$$

**Note:** Unless otherwise stated, all restaurants accept credit cards and serve vegetarian meals

Left **La Citadelle** Right **Marché du Vieux-Port**

# Québec City

EUROPEANS FIRST SETTLED HERE IN 1608, *and throughout its 400-year history Québec City has been the focus of political struggle between the British and the French – a battle that still rages today in this home of French separatism. Yet despite this turmoil, with its beautiful riverside setting, heritage sites, and cobblestone streets – all of which earned it World Heritage status in 1985 – the city is a traveler's dream. Poised upon the Cap Diamant escarpment overlooking both the St Lawrence River and les Laurentides, the city is home to a Francophone population rich in cultural pride and exuberance, magnificent architecture, preserved churches and monuments, fine cuisine and numerous opportunities for outdoor adventure.*

## TOP 10 Sights

1. La Citadelle
2. Musée de la Civilisation de Québec
3. Parc des Champs-de-Bataille
4. Château Frontenac
5. Place Royale
6. Observatoire de la capitale
7. Quartier Petit-Champlain
8. Marché du Vieux-Port
9. Place de l'Hôtel de Ville
10. Faubourg Saint-Jean-Baptiste

Quartier Petit-Champlain

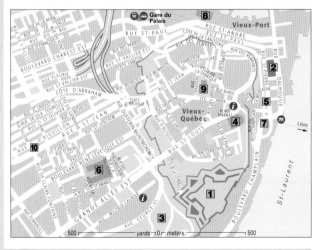

### La Citadelle

Strategically perched on the precipice of Cap Diamant with a full 360-degree view, this powerful bastion would daunt the bravest of enemies approaching the riverside city. All you need to do is attend one of its summertime cannon-firing demonstrations to appreciate the persuasive power of this mighty fortress *(see pp22–3)*.

### Musée de la Civilisation de Québec

Architect Moishe Safdie mirrored the surrounding neighborhood by incorporating the French Regime style in his design for this interesting building. Inside, however, it is another story – a futuristic world complete with a range of interactive exhibitions, as well as displays of folk art, religious icons, antique furniture in period settings, and everyday items that illustrate life in the city during its 400-year history. There are also collaborative exhibitions at Place Royale and the Musée de l'Amérique française, the additional space allowing for a more comprehensive program covering multiple themes and generations *(see pp24–5)*.

Musée de la Civilisation de Québec façade

Military Drill Hall, Parc des Champs-de-Bataille

### Parc des Champs-de-Bataille

Located inside a former jail now called the Baillairgé Pavilion, the Battlefields Park Interpretation Center presents an inventive agenda to illustrate one of North America's most historic sites. The highlight is a multimedia show recounting the battles of 1759 and 1760 that took place here, leading to a French defeat by the British *(see p32)*. An imposing mural by Québec artist Aline Martineau also illustrates the establishment of the park in the 1930s and how it has changed over the 20th century *(see p37)*. ◈ Map K6 • Open 10am–5:30pm daily (closed Mon Oct–May) • Adm

### Château Frontenac

The most photographed landmark in the city, this imposing hotel with its green copper roof is an architectural jewel designed by architect Bruce Price as a French-style château. Since it opened in 1893, the hotel has welcomed the rich, the famous and the noble through its doors and into its plush salons. Guided tours are available *(see p112)*.

### Trompe-l'Oeil

*Trompe-l'oeil* means "to deceive the eye" and if you are in the Quartier Saint-Roch district of the city (near the train station) you can see a marvelous example of this art tradition on the columns on rue Charest Est. Combining the energetic talents of street graffiti artists under the guidance of a trained painter, a project evolved creating *trompe l'oeil* paintings to decorate cement highway pillars. The results are astounding and have led to the graffiti artists forming their own legitimate company.

### Place Royale

The site of Nouvelle-France's first settlement, built by Samuel de Champlain in 1608, has been the hub of the city's cultural activities throughout its history. Shipbuilders, merchants, clergy and everyday citizens once gathered here to conduct commerce, celebrate harvests, marry, drink and bury their dead. Today, festivals such as Les Fêtes de la Nouvelle-France *(see p43)* rekindle the days of the early settlers with theatrical performances incorporating period costumes and traditional music. Don't miss Église Notre-Dame-des-Victoires with its paintings by Van Dyck depicting French victory over the British in 1690. ◈ *Map M5*

**Place Royale**

### Observatoire de la capitale

From the 31st floor of the Capital Observatory you can enjoy spectacular views of the entire region. Adding to the experience are the taped interpretation guides offering information about the city in French, English and Spanish. Many city tours begin or end here. ◈ *1037 rue de la Chevrotière • Map J6 • Open 10am–5pm daily (closed Mon mid-Oct–mid-Jun) • Dis. access • Adm*

### Quartier Petit-Champlain

Home to artisans in the 17th century and dockworkers in the 19th century, the houses in this area have now been renovated and adapted into a range of eclectic gift shops, turning what is the oldest part of the city into today's liveliest quarter. Maple butter, French macramé, and sculpted cherrywood cribs are just a few of the many unusual treats you can purchase here. Along the way you can eat and drink in the bars and cafés lining the pedestrianized streets. ◈ *Map M5*

### Marché du Vieux-Port

The Bassin Louise is the home of the Old Town's fresh produce market, where farmers from Ile d'Orléans *(see pp28–9)* and other outlying areas bring their harvest to tempt appetites and inspire local chefs. Don't be afraid to ask for a sample before you buy, especially at Le Fromageur cheese stall. Inside the green-roofed building is a café, where you can savor more of the local delights. ◈ *160 quai St-André • Map L4*

### Place de l'Hôtel de Ville

In the 18th century this square was the site of the Notre-Dame market and is still a popular gathering place for locals. During the summer it is often jammed with visitors who come to enjoy free music concerts and performances by local actors. The Romanesque architecture, as seen in the Hôtel de Ville (town hall) immediately beside the square, lends the area an imposing air. ✏ Map L5

**Porte Saint-Jean**

### Faubourg Saint-Jean-Baptiste

Built as a military defence against the British in the 18th century, the striking stone gate (Porte Saint-Jean) is now a tourist draw from which visitors can access and walk for 4 km (3 miles) along the city's ramparts. The area around the gate, also known as Quartier Montcalm, has an intense concentration of Québécois specialty merchants, as well as designer boutiques, cultural outlets and nightclubs. Bring your appetite too, because this zone is famous for its bistros and restaurants serving fine French cuisine. ✏ Map H5

## A Day Exploring the Old Town

### Morning

Start your day at **Château Frontenac** *(see p89)* for a breathtaking view of the St Lawrence River, Basse-Ville, Vieux-Port and **Île d'Orléans** *(see pp28–9)* in the distance. Immediately beside the hotel runs **Terrasse-Dufferin** *(see p93)*, a boardwalk clinging to the rock escarpment complete with ornate Parisian-style street lamps. After taking in the exhilarating surroundings, stroll through the Jardins des Gouverneurs and look for monuments to Wolfe and Montcalm, generals in the Battle of the Plains of Abraham *(see p32)*.

Go back along Terrasse-Dufferin to **Quartier Petit-Champlain**, the oldest merchant district in North America, with a dazzling variety of boutiques and souvenir shops.

Enjoy a mouthwatering seafood lunch at **Le Marie-Clarisse** *(see p99)*.

### Afternoon

If you want to stretch your legs after lunch, follow the natural flow of the land to the waterfront, head left along rue Dalhousie and the Vieux-Port and turn left at rue St-André. Here you'll find the delights of **Marché du Vieux-Port**, where you could easily spend the rest of the afternoon, sampling the local treats.

For an early evening drink, there is no better spot to finish your tour than the Aviatic Club bar/restaurant in the elegant train station *(450 rue de la Gare-du-Palais • Map K4)*.

Left **Porte Saint-Louis** Right **Hôtel du Parlement**

# Best of the Rest

### Porte Saint-Louis
Although the city walls were a security necessity in the 18th century, they were an impediment to merchants, so large gates such as Porte Saint-Louis were cut into the fortifications to improve the flow of commerce. ◉ Map K5

### Centre d'initiation aux fortifications et à la Poudrière de l'Esplanade
On display here are scale models and documents tracing the history of the city's defense network. ◉ 97 rue St-Louis • Map K5 • Open mid-May–mid-Oct: 10am–5pm daily • Adm

### Sanctuaire Notre-Dame du Sacré-Coeur
Stained-glass windows and marble plaques testifying to favors received through prayer are highlights of this Neo-Gothic jewel, built in 1910. ◉ 71, rue Ste-Ursule • Map L5 • Open 7am–8pm daily • Free

### Musée de cire de Québec
Life-size wax figures welcome you at this 17th-century house – historical personalities are on the ground floor, with contemporary stars upstairs. ◉ 22 rue Ste-Anne • Map L5 • Open May–Oct: 9am–9pm daily; Nov–Apr: 10am–5pm daily • Adm

### Centre d'interprétation de la vie urbaine
Québec City's history is interpreted in 12 multimedia segments covering events from 1608 until the present. ◉ 43 côte de la Fabrique • Map L4 • Open 10am–5pm daily • Free

### Hôtel du Parlement
The city's political forum takes place here. ◉ 1045 rue des Parlementaires • Map K5 • Open 10am–5pm daily • Free

### Maison Chevalier
This former inn, built in 1792, houses displays on 17th- and 18th-century Québec. ◉ 50 rue de Marché Champlain • Map M5 • Open Jun–Sep: 9:30am–5pm Tue–Sun; Oct–Apr: 10am–10pm Sat–Sun • Free

### Musée Bon-Pasteur
Highlighting the activities of the Soeurs du Bon-Pasteur religious order. ◉ 14 rue Couillard • Map L4 • Open 1–5pm Tue–Sun • Free

### Québec Experience
Animatronics and holograms are used to explore over 400 years of life in the city. ◉ 8 rue du Trésor • Map L5 • Open May–Oct: 10am–10pm daily; Oct–May: 10am–5pm daily • Adm

### Ferry, Québec City to Lévis
This 10-minute crossing offers a stunning view of the city. ◉ 10 rue des Traversiers • Map M5

Share your travel recommendations on traveldk.com

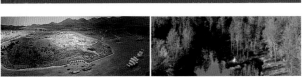

Left **Diorama, Musée du Fort** Right **Parc National de la Jacques-Cartier**

# 🔟 Further Attractions

### 1 Musée du Fort
State-of-the-art technology has created a diorama that illustrates the tale of this walled city. ✪ 10 rue Ste-Anne • Map L5 • Open 10am–5pm daily • Adm

### 2 Musée d'art Inuit Brousseau
The Inuit sculptures displayed here help illustrate the lifestyles and traditions of these native Canadian peoples. ✪ 39 rue St-Louis • Map K6 • Open 9:30am–5pm daily • Adm • www.artinuit.ca

### 3 Bastion du Roy Lookout
Come here for incredible views of Ile d'Orléans, the St Lawrence River, Mont Sainte-Anne and the South Shore. ✪ End of rue de la Porte • Map L5

### 4 Parks Canada Exhibition Hall
Set in a 19th-century heritage building, this site presents temporary cultural exhibitions and offers brochures and descriptions of Parks Canada sites throughout Québec and Canada. ✪ 3 rue Buade • Map L5 • Open 8:30am–4:30pm daily • Free

### 5 Les Glissades de la Terrasse-Dufferin
This unique winter attraction features three icy toboggan runs bolting participants at 70 kmph (45 mph) down a steep 250-m (820-ft) incline. A Québec tradition. ✪ Map L5 • Open mid-Dec–mid-Mar: 11am–11pm daily • Adm

### 6 Verrerie la Mailloche
A glass-blowing museum and shop where you can see masters of this craft at work. ✪ 58 rue Sous-le-Fort • Map M5 • Open 10am–noon, 1–4:30pm Wed–Sun • Adm

### 7 Grand canyon des Chutes Sainte-Anne
Only 20 minutes outside the city is a series of waterfalls contained in a narrow canyon. A breathtaking sight. ✪ Route 138 est, Beaupré • Map P3 • Dis. access • Adm

### 8 Chemin du Roy
The "King's Road" (route 138) winds from Montréal to Québec. It is known today by cyclists as the Route Verte for its beautiful bike path trailing beside the St Lawrence River. ✪ Map P3

### 9 Parc National de la Jacques-Cartier
Located 40 km (25 miles) from downtown Québec City, this immense park abounds with lakes, mountains, and outdoor activities in all seasons. ✪ 325 chemin du Hibou, Stoneham • Map P2

### 10 Station Touristique Duchesnay
To see the glorious Canadian forests head west toward Sainte-Catherine-de-la-Jacques-Cartier. This region has the Hôtel de Glace (see p45), and a riot of winter attractions, as well as watersports on Lac Saint-Joseph. ✪ 143 route Duchesnay, Sainte Catherine de la Jacques Cartier • Map N3

Left **Rue du Petit-Champlain** Right **Fresh produce, Marché du Vieux-Port**

# 🔟 Shopping and Markets

### 1 Simons
Fashions for the whole family can be purchased here, accompanied by impeccable service from the staff. ◎ *20 côte de la Fabrique • Map L4 • Dis. access*

### 2 Rue du Petit-Champlain
A marvelous pedestrianized shopping concourse features fashion boutiques, souvenir shops, restaurants, art galleries, theaters and a park. Don't miss a ride on the Funiculaire *(see p90)*.

### 3 Galeries de la Capitale
One of the busiest shopping malls in the country with over 250 stores offering fashion, electronics, groceries, books, furniture and more. A theme area for children includes a ferris wheel, roller coaster and skating rink. ◎ *5401 blvd des Galeries, off rte 310 • Dis. access*

### 4 Place Québec
Just outside Porte Kent, this bustling complex is the home of up-scale shops, restaurants and cinemas. ◎ *880 autoroute Dufferin-Montmorency • Dis. access*

### 5 Place de la Cité
Southwest of town you will find shopper's heaven where three upscale malls converge. It has the largest concentration of exclusive boutiques in Québec, and also features a produce market and restaurants. ◎ *2600 blvd Laurier, junction of hwys 175 and 720, Sainte-Foy • Dis. access*

### 6 Marché du Vieux-Port
This farmers' market is a cornucopia of the finest produce grown in the province *(see p90)*.

### 7 J.-A. Moisan
Jean-Alfred's establishment began in 1871, making it the oldest grocery store in North America. Typical articles on sale include fine condiments, meat, bread and pastries, and cheeses from around the world. ◎ *699 rue St-Jean • Map J5 • Dis. access.*

### 8 Les Promenades du Vieux-Québec
This tiny shopping cluster features the Québec Experience movie on the second floor *(see p92)* and the charming Au Royaume de Père Noël, where you can buy unusual Christmas decorations throughout the year. ◎ *43 rue Buade • Map L5*

### 9 Marché Public de Sainte-Foy
A mix between an age-old farmers' market and a contemporary grocery store. Being able to meet the grower face to face offers a satisfying assurance of the freshness of your purchases. ◎ *939 ave Rolande-Beaudin, Sainte-Foy • Rte 440*

### 10 La Carotte Joyeuse
Specialists in organically grown produce. Also tempting baked goods as well as aromatic and medicinal herbs and spices. ◎ *690 rue St-Jean • Map J5*

Left **Théâtre Petit-Champlain** Right **Le Dag**

# ⁵⁰ Nightlife

### Grand Théâtre de Québec
The Grand Théâtre showcases the talents of l'Orchestre Symphonique de Québec, Opéra de Québec and an international line-up of musical stars *(see p41)*. ◈ *269 blvd René-Lévesque Est • Map H6 • Dis. access*

### Le Pape Georges
Enjoy live music (mostly jazz and blues) from Thursdays to Sundays while sampling local cheeses and cold meats with a wide selection of wines by the glass. ◈ *8¼ rue Cul-de-Sac • Map M5*

### Palais Montcalm
This multi-room theater offers the biggest names in music, as well as a smaller, more intimate space for emerging artists. ◈ *995 place d'Youville • Map L5*

### L'Inox
A blessing for beer lovers is this micro-brewery in the city's Vieux-Port. The place has a clear passion for the stuff and offers a wide selection of home-made blondes, whites, ambers, reds and browns. ◈ *655 Grande Allée Est • Map J6*

### Le Dag
A large, popular three-storied club. A live band venue on the ground floor evolves upstairs into a more conventional disco. The action does not begin until after midnight. There's also a cigar lounge. ◈ *600 rue Grande Allée Est • Map J6 • Dis. access*

### Chez Maurice Complex
Competing with Le Dag across the street is another wild, three-tiered entertainment tower. Chez Charlotte's lounge is on the top floor, with the dance club Chez Maurice and smoking club Société Cigares below. ◈ *575 rue Grande Allée Est • Map J6 • Dis. access*

### Le Boudoir Lounge
This trendy venue with a busy, vibrating dancefloor has an impressive LED light system. ◈ *441 rue du Parvis • Map J6*

### Théâtre de la Bordée
Founded in 1976, this attractive theater stages a range of classical and contemporary performances from poetry to Shakespeare, with sets designed by luminaries such as Robert Lepage *(see p39)*. ◈ *315 rue St-Joseph Est • Map H4 • Dis. access*

### Théâtre Petit-Champlain
One of the best small theatres in North America for design, ambiance, repertoire and location. Evocative performances of music, song, dance and modern art. ◈ *78 rue du Petit-Champlain • Map M5 • Dis. access*

### Le Temps Partiel
French and English punk, goth, techno-goth, and indie bands play at this alternative club where local art adorns the walls. DJs and dancing on Fridays. ◈ *698 rue d'Aiguillon • Map J5*

Left **Kookening Kafe** Right **Pub d'Orsay**

# Bars and Cafés

### 1 Kookening Kafe
Play board games or relax in this trendy, student-populated and inexpensive café, where tandoori and Tex-Mex specialties blend with New Age jazz. ◈ *565 rue St-Jean • Map J5 • Dis. access*

### 2 Le Ninkasi du Faubourg
Named after the ancient Sumerian goddess of beer, this microbrewery also doubles as a live music venue and art gallery. ◈ *811 rue St-Jean • Map J5*

### 3 Pub d'Orsay
Without a doubt, one of the most appealing pubs, indoors or out, for Québec's famous micro-brewery beers such as Belle Gueule, Boréale and Blanche de Chambly, and the unique taste of Cidre de Minot. ◈ *65 rue Buade • Map L5 • Dis. access*

### 4 Pub Thomas Dunn
This classic English pub has a winning formula: sumptuous mahogany decor, an extensive beer list, the best fish and chips in town and a location directly across from the train station. ◈ *369 rue St-Paul • Map K4 • Dis. access*

### 5 Café Krieghoff
If you wish to venture into the heart of Québec City's artistic community, there is no better place than a seat at this convivial café. Light meals and strong coffee. B&B accommo-dations too. ◈ *1091 ave Cartier • Bus No. 10*

### 6 Buffet de l'Antiquaire
Come to this busy diner for hearty helpings of traditional comfort food such as pea soup or meat pie. Lumberjack break-fasts, with meats, eggs, fries, beans, and toast, are popular too. ◈ *95 rue St-Paul • Map K4*

### 7 The Dazibo
A magical mix of an Irish pub and a French kitchen makes this charming eatery worth a side trip out of town. Try their hearty Irish stew and delicious desserts. ◈ *58 rue Duchesnay, Sainte-Catherine-de-la-Jacques-Cartier • Map P3*

### 8 La Barbarie
Highlights of this eco-friendly brewery include a tasting room and a beer garden. This is an excellent place to sample the locally made beer. ◈ *310 rue St-Roch • Map J4*

### 9 Chez Temporel
This popular meeting place has the best homemade croissants, *croque-monsieurs* and coffee in the province. ◈ *25 rue Couillard • Map L4*

### 10 Le Cercle
This bar has extra tables on "catwalks" overlooking a small dancefloor. The chef creates *tapas*, specialty menus for special occasions, and other offerings showcasing regional ingredients. There is an art gallery in the basement. ◈ *228 rue St-Joseph Est • Map J4*

**Price Categories**

For a three-course meal for one with a glass of house wine, and all unavoidable extra charges including tax.

| | |
|---|---|
| **$** | under $20 |
| **$$** | $20–$35 |
| **$$$** | $35–$60 |
| **$$$$** | $60–$85 |
| **$$$$$** | over $85 |

Above **Café de la Terrasse**

# 🔟 Restaurants

### L'Échaudé
Locals coming to this contemporary bistro ask for the wine recommendations to be paired with inventive appetizers or order the perfectly done steaks. ◉ 73 rue Sault-au-Matelot • Map M4 • (418) 692 1299 • Dis. access • $$

### Café de la Terrasse
This café is located in the Fairmont Château Frontenac (see p112). Choose from their scrumptious buffets featuring fabulous selections of regional foods. ◉ 1 rue des Carrières • Map L5 • (418) 692 3861 • Dis. access • $$$

### Le Bonaparte
French cuisine is expertly served in this 1832 heritage house. Try the venison or the seared scallops. Murder Mystery soirées are held at weekends. ◉ 680 Grande Allée Est • Map J6 • (418) 647 4747 • Dis. access • $$$

### Charbon Bar & Grill
The tantalizing aroma of meat over an open grill wafts through the Gare du Palais station which houses this popular steakhouse. ◉ 450 rue de la Gare-du-Palais • Map K4 • (418) 522 0133 • Dis. access • $$$

### Café du Monde
Step inside this bistro, with its waterside location and great food, and you could imagine yourself in Paris itself. Try black pudding with apple compote. ◉ 84 rue Dalhousie • Map M5 • (418) 692 4455 • Dis. access • $$$

### Pub St-Patrick
A cozy, authentic Irish pub with a spectacular patio in summer. ◉ 45 rue Couillard (off rue St-Jean) • Map L4 • (418) 521 1885 • $$

### 47e Parallèle Resto International
European-style dishes fine-tuned by the owner/chef. ◉ 333 St Amable • Map L5 • (418) 692 1534 • $$$$

### Le Marie-Clarisse
This gourmet haven prepares seafood and meat in creative ways. ◉ 12 rue du Petit-Champlain • Map M5 • (418) 692 0857 • $$$$

### Le Saint-Amour
An amazing menu includes caribou steak and guinea fowl with wild mushrooms. ◉ 48 rue Ste-Ursule • Map K5 • (418) 694 0667 • Dis. access • $$$

### Le Lapin Sauté
The French country fare at this charming bistro includes rabbit-centric dishes such as rabbit pie. ◉ 52 rue du Petit-Champlain • Map M5 • (418) 692 5325 • $$

**Note:** Unless otherwise stated, all restaurants accept credit cards and serve vegetarian meals

Left **Basilique Sainte-Anne-de-Beaupré** Right **Chocolate-maker, Ile d'Orléans**

# 🔟 Excursions from Québec City

### 1 Basilique Sainte-Anne-de-Beaupré
This mammoth cathedral site is busy throughout the year with religious pilgrims, following the legacy of answered prayers touted by those who have visited this beautiful shrine (see pp26–7).

### 2 Ile d'Orléans
This enchanting island outside Québec City is dotted with quaint farms that produce many of the fruits, vegetables and culinary specialties of the region. Designated a heritage site with over 600 preserved buildings, visiting Ile d'Orléans is a memorable experience (see pp28–9).

### 3 Parc de la Chute-Montmorency
When the first settlers crossed the Atlantic and sailed up the St Lawrence River to this virgin area, they were greeted by the

**Parc de la Chute-Montmorency**

sight of these powerful waterfalls, which, at 83 m (272 ft), are higher than Niagara. Ride the cable car to the top and visit Manoir Montmorency (1781), with its interpretation center, boutiques, restaurant and terrace with a view of the action. Other vantage points are also scattered about the park (see p28). ⬚ 2490 ave Royale, Hwy 138 east • Map P3

### 4 Mont Sainte-Anne
A sensational outdoor playground 40 km (25 miles) east of Québec City, the mountain is one of the most popular destinations for world-class skiing, paragliding, mountain biking or golfing at the 18-hole Le Grand Vallon course. With over 200 km (125 miles) of hiking trails, which double in the winter as paths for snowshoeing, dog-sledding and cross-country skiing, Mont Sainte-Anne defines perfectly the four-season personality of the province. ⬚ 2000 blvd Beau-Pré, Beaupré • Map P3

### 5 Cap Tourmente
You can see an incredible congregation of wild birds indigenous to the province by driving 45 minutes east of Québec City. Over 290 species populate the marshes, lowlands and hills of the area, the most photographed being the snow goose – thousands of them return to these fertile grounds every year. ⬚ 570 chemin du Cap-Tourmente • Map P3 • Dis. access

**Grosse Ile chapel**

### 6 Grosse Ile and Irish Memorial National Historic Site

These sites commemorate the tragic events experienced by many Irish immigrants who, escaping the potato famine in their native country, were quarantined here on their arrival to Canada but died during the typhoid epidemic of 1847. Take the tourist trolley to the village and hospitals sector, where you can admire numerous historic buildings, and visit the restored 1847 Lazaretto Catholic chapel. *Map P3*

### 7 Charlevoix

Nowhere is the spirit and passion of Québec Province more obvious than in this 200-km (130-mile) coastal district of rolling hills, quaint villages and pastoral scenes. Baie St-Paul, with its heritage houses, is one of the most charming. *Map P2*

### 8 Tadoussac

Tadoussac is whale country – whalers were here even before the European explorers, comprising the first white settlement north of Mexico. Visitors can take boat trips out to view the minke, grey and beluga whales in the Saguenay-St Lawrence Marine Park. *Map Q1 • Boat trips: Croisières Dufour; (1 800) 463 5250*

### 9 Saguenay and Lac Saint-Jean

The only fjord in North America, leading inland to Lac Saint-Jean, is a designated protected area because it is frequented by beluga whales, dolphins, black bear, moose, and many other varieties of wildlife. Granite walls over 300 m (985 ft) high cast a mysterious and powerful aura over the maritime environment and give rise to the fables and legends associated with the movement of its ocean tides. *Map Q1 • Parc national du Saguenay: 91 Notre-Dame, Rivière-Éternité*

### 10 Parc des Hautes-Gorges-de-la-Rivière-Malbaie

This national park is one of Québec's most beautiful natural monuments. Steep slopes, beautiful natural surroundings, and the unusual course of the Malbaie river make this site unique. The point where the river valley takes a sharp 90-degree turn is a protected UNESCO area. Walk through the valley or in the summer, join a guided cruise along the calm waters. You can also stay at the park overnight. *Access via St-Aimé-des-Lacs on rue Principale • Map P2 • Open May–Oct daily • www.sepaq.com*

# STREETSMART

MONTRÉAL & QUÉBEC CITY'S TOP 10

Left **Centre Infotouriste** Right **Québec City and Area Tourism and Convention Bureau**

Streetsmart

# 🔟 Planning Your Trip

### When To Go
Early summer and fall are the best times to visit Quebec, when the climate is more temperate. However, if you are interested in the variety of winter sports on offer in the province plan your visit in October to November or January to March.

### Peak Seasons
Christmas can be magical in both cities, but as a result they are crowded with tourists who come to celebrate amid the fairylights and the snow. June and July are the main months for the region's renowned festivals *(see pp42–3)*, so these months are also frenetic, but fun. Québec City draws the crowds to its Carnaval each February *(see pp44–5)*.

### Tourist Offices

**Tourisme Montréal**
*1001 Sq Dorchester*
*• (514) 844 5400 • www. tourisme-montreal.org*

**Centre Infotouriste**
*1001 Sq Dorchester*
*• (514) 873 2015*

**Québec City and Area Tourism and Convention Bureau**
*(418) 641 6654*
*• www.quebecregion. com*

**Ministry of Tourism for Québec**
*www.bonjourquebec. com*

### What to Pack
The term "weather extremes" might have been invented in Quebec, where residents and visitors alike comment on variations from hour to hour. Temperatures range from 40° C (105° F) in summer to -40° C (-40° F) during winter ice storms. Packing rain gear is *de rigueur* and wearing layers of clothes that can be taken on and off is a sensible option.

### Passports & Visas
To enter Canada American citizens, like all other visitors, must have a valid passport that extends beyond the length of the trip (likewise, to enter America all visitors require a passport). You may stay in the country for up to six months, providing your passport covers this period. US and EU citizens need no visa to enter Canada, but other nationalities should check at the Canadian Embassy or Consulate in their home country for up-to-date regulations.

### Travel Insurance
Health care is expensive in North America so it is essential to take out travel insurance prior to departure to avoid paying high fees should you fall ill during your trip. Make sure the insurance also covers travel cancellations as well as loss of valuables should you be the victim of theft.

### Airlines
More than 50 airlines serve Montréal and Québec City, but the scheduled airline with the most international flights is Air Canada. The charter company Air Transat offers cheaper options *(see p106)*.

### Customs
You are forbidden to bring certain food products, such as fruit, into Canada from abroad and sniffer dogs may operate at airports to check your luggage. Visitors over the age of 18 may import 200 cigarettes, 50 cigars, one liter of spirits and 1.5 liters of wine.

### Time Zones
Québec is 5 hours behind Greenwich Mean Time (GMT) – the same time zone as New York City. When it is midday in Montréal, it will be 5pm in London, 9am in Los Angeles and 3am in Sydney.

### Electricity
The whole of North America operates on a 110-volt, 60-cycle electrical system, with two- or three-pronged plugs. Equipment manufactured in other countries will need an adaptor.

### Maps
Maps of both cities as well as a Montréal Métro and bus service map are available from tourist offices.

*Sign up for DK's email newsletter on traveldk.com*

Left **Airport taxi** Right **Cobblestone streets, Montréal**

# 🔟 Things to Avoid

### 1 Airport Taxis
The airport taxi system is convenient but the airport bus, operated by Aéroports de Montréal (ADM), is much cheaper, running to the center of the city from 7am until 1am. There is also a shuttle in Québec City.

### 2 Bridges at Rush-Hour
The best way to deal with rush-hour traffic on the 11 commuter bridges in Montréal is to avoid it. From 4:30pm to 6:30pm traffic is at a standstill. In the morning, wait until after 9:30am before driving. Québec City's concern is the Pierre-Laporte and Ile d'Orléans bridges. The same advice applies to these.

### 3 Driving in Cities
Unless driving through a maze of construction re-routings, one-way streets, closed-due-to-festival signs and pumped-up summer traffic is your idea of a good time, do yourself a favor and use public transportation, taxis, walk or rent a bike. In winter you also have the ice, snow banks, poor visibility and less street parking to consider.

### 4 High-Heel Shoes in Vieux-Montréal
A word of warning to fashionistas: walking through the ancient cobbled streets of Old Town areas in high-heeled footwear is a sure way of canceling the next day of activities. Make sure you wear sturdy, comfortable footwear.

### 5 Airport Bureaux de Change
The rates at airport exchangers are famously poor the world over. It is always preferable to deal with specialists in currency exchange in the cities themselves.

### 6 Pickpockets
A pickpocket looks like any other person, so be watchful of characters bumping into you – it could be a thief at work. A favorite trick of pickpockets is to work the crowds during the area's many festivals so be particularly careful at these events.

### 7 Dangerous areas
Montréal and Québec City are famously safe cities but there are areas to avoid. Stay away from Pascal Street in Montréal Nord, east of boulevard Pie-IX, as well as rue Ontario Est – plan your visit during daylight. The Côtes-des-Neiges neighborhood, especially Barclay Avenue, is also a no-go area at night but fine during the day. Strip clubs abound in the province and seedier elements are constant in these establishments. Québec City is very safe but common sense must be exercised.

### 8 Airport Con Artists
Montréal International Airport has had its share of organized gang-related con artists preying on the public. While authorities have stepped up security, be aware of your possessions at all times. One of the favorite ruses is to distract your attention while stealing your luggage. They customarily work in teams of two or three, so monitor your luggage attentively at all times.

### 9 Street Beggars
Montréal and Québec City have street beggars who congregate in high-traffic areas and outside SAQ stores, the province-run alcohol outlets. However, the province is a world leader in providing hostel facilities, free meals, medical services and halfway houses for the homeless, so beggars do have other options beyond your cash donation, which may be worth bearing in mind.

### 10 Hotel Telephone Calls
Avoid long-distance calls charged directly to hotel bills – they are at least three times the price of using a phone card. Buy one of the pre-paid phone cards available at convenience stores and newsstands. The other option is to contact the international operator of your contact country.

Left **Pierre Elliott Trudeau International Airport** Right **Gare Centrale, Montréal**

# Getting to Montréal & Québec City

### 1 By Air to Montréal

Visitors arriving by air will land at Pierre Elliott Trudeau International Airport, where transportation to central Montréal can be arranged. From here you can also make connecting flights to other Canadian and foreign cities, as well as other regions of Québec Province. Montréal has a second airport called Mirabel used for vacation charters and cargo flights. ✪ *Aéroports de Montréal: (514) 394 7377 • www.admtl.com*

### 2 By Air to Québec City

Jean Lesage International Airport is located about 15 minutes from Québec City and is serviced by several major US airlines, a Cuban carrier, Air Canada and Air Transat, a charter company with direct flights to Paris. ✪ *Aéroport de Québec City • (418) 640 2700 • www. aeroportdequebec.com*

### 3 By Train to Montréal

Gare Centrale is where the Amtrak trains arrive from the US and VIA trains pull in from other points in Canada. This is also where you connect to buses for Québec City and daily services for other Canadian cities. ✪ *VIA Rail Canada Reservations: (514) 989-2626; www.via.ca • Amtrak: 1-800-USA-RAIL*

### 4 By Cruise Ship to Montréal

Cruise ships arriving in the Port of Montréal anchor at the Iberville Terminal, within walking distance of Vieux-Montréal. Arriving in Montréal by cruise ship, gracefully sailing under the Jacques Cartier Bridge and into Vieux-Montréal, is a romantic introduction to the "Paris of the Americas." ✪ *Old Port offices: (514) 496 7678*

### 5 By Cruise Ship to Québec City

Within walking distance of the Vieux-Port, the cruise terminal welcomes the floating hotels into the city. Traditionally, the cruise season extends from April to October. ✪ *www.portquebec.ca*

### 6 By Road

To reach Montréal by car use either Hwy 401 from southern Ontario, which becomes Hwy 20 at the Québec border, and cross the Pont Galipeau bridge, or take Hwy 40 from Ottawa which crosses the Pont Ile aux Tourtres. The Cantons de l'Est autoroute (Hwy 10) is fed by US freeways 91 and 93, with other US East Coast travelers using Hwy 15 – both of these lead to Pont Champlain. Québec City visitors can choose either Hwy 20 or Hwy 40, both from Montréal, or Hwy 138 if traveling to Québec City from the east.

### 7 By Bus to Montréal

Many bus routes connect Montréal to Northern Québec, the Maritimes, Ontario, and New England. The city's bus station is at the intersection of three métro lines in eastern downtown. ✪ *Station Centrale: 505 blvd de Maisonneuve, (514) 842 2281*

### 8 By Ferry to Montréal

Since Montréal is an island city, shuttle boats *(navettes)* are in use, but only in fair weather, which fluctuates according to the winter icepack. A shuttle service is available from the South Shore community of Longueuil, generally from the end of May until mid-October. ✪ *Navettes: (514) 281 8000*

### 9 By Ferry to Québec City

One of the best viewpoints of this city is from the ferry crossing to the town of Lévis on the south shore of the St Lawrence River (see p92). ✪ *Ferry schedules and information: (418) 837 2408*

### 10 By Bus to Québec City

There are two major bus stations serving Québec City, one under the Gare Centrale station in the old town, and the other in Sainte-Foy. ✪ *Gare du Palais: 320 rue Abraham-Martin • Ste-Foy: 925 ave de Rochebelle*

Left **Cycling in Montréal** Right **Calèche ride**

# TOP 10 Getting Around Montréal & Québec City

## 1 Montréal Métro
The best way around Montréal is by Métro, which operates from 5:30am until 1am. Québec City has no Métro. ⑨ www.stm.info

## 2 By Bus
Montréal's bus/Métro system acts as a single network seven days a week. A single fare allows access to the entire system. Buses also run efficiently in Québec City. ⑨ Montréal buses: www.stm.info • Québec City buses: (418) 627 2511; www.rtcquebec.ca

## 3 Tickets
The same tickets are valid on both the Métro and buses in Montréal. If you plan to use public transportation frequently during your stay, it is worthwhile investing in a one-day Carte Touristique for $9.00 or a three-day pass for $17.00 and you will have unlimited access to the major areas. These cards are available at the Berri-UQAM and Bonaventure Métro stations and, during the summer, at the Sherbrooke, Mont-Royal, Pie-IX, Viau, Jean-Talon and Longueuil stations too.

## 4 By Car
The Province of Québec has a reputation of being a combination of fast drivers, one-way streets, complicated parking signs, short-lived meters and over-priced parking lots. Overnight indoor parking or taking taxis are both worth the investment while staying in either city.

## 5 On Foot
Both cities are walker-friendly, providing many wonderful streets to wander along and places to stop for a break. There are clearly marked walking trails but they share space with cyclists and sometimes in-line skaters, so be careful, but courteous.

## 6 Cycling
Cyclists abound throughout Québec on the city streets, bike paths and in the parks. With over 350 km (215 miles) of paths around Montréal too, there is no shortage of surface. Ça Roule is a rental and repair shop. ⑨ Ça Roule: 27 rue de la Commune Est • (514) 866 0633 • www.caroulemontreal.com

## 7 Taxis
For under $10 you can get from one place to another in the downtown core of both cities, rush-hour traffic notwithstanding.

## 8 Calèche Rides
In Montréal, calèche rides (horse-drawn carriages) are available at Place d'Armes, Place Jacques-Cartier, the foot of boulevard St-Laurent or by calling Lucky Luc. In Québec City, call Calèches du Vieux-Québec or hail one on any of the old town streets. It's a romantic, if expensive, way to get around. Rates are the same in the two cities, roughly $60.00 per hour, but each driver negotiates separately. ⑨ Lucky Luc: (514) 934 6105 • Calèches du Vieux-Québec: (418) 683 9222

## 9 By Boat
For the best view of Vieux-Montréal, hire a boat – the Vieux-Port has all the relevant information. Other beautiful areas to anchor include Marina de la Ronde and Lachine's Pleasure Craft Harbour and Visitors' Marina. ⑨ Vieux-Port: (514) 496 7678; www.oldportof montreal.com • Marina de la Ronde: Parc Jean-Drapeau, (514) 875 0111• Pleasure Craft Harbour and Visitors' Marina: (514) 634 0646

## 10 Transport for the Disabled
Both cities have partial disabled access to their public transportation. Montréal International Airport is equipped with disabled service personnel and equipment; transport from Québec City airport can be arranged by calling Roy & Morin. STCUM, Montréal's transportation authority, also provides special vans for wheelchair passengers. ⑨ Roy & Morin: (418) 622 6566 • STCUM: (514) 786 4636; www.stcum.qc.ca

Left **Bureau de Change** Right **Newspaper store**

# Banking and Communications

### Currency
Quebecers use the Canadian dollar ($) which is made up of 100 cents (¢). A 5 cent piece is called a nickel, a 10 cent piece a dime, and a 25 cent piece a quarter. The $1 coin has a loon (a type of waterfowl) on it so is known as a loonie; the $2 coin is known as a toonie. French Canadians refer to *sous* meaning penny or *piastres* for dollar. Paper money comes in 5, 10, 20, 50 and 100-dollar denominations.

### Bureaux de Change
These money-changing shops cash checks and exchange currencies provided you have sufficient identification. For cash currency exchanges they sometimes provide better rates than banks. You can find them at airports, hotels and on popular boulevards and squares.

### Caisses Populaires
In the earlier 1900s Quebecers opened the first credit union in North America called a *caisses populaire*, or people's bank. Today, while not as numerous as banks, they are more amiable and give attractive rates.

### Credit and Debit Cards
Quebecers recognize all major credit cards issued by legitimate financial entities throughout the world, but prefer cash, as there are charges associated with plastic. Bank debit cards are common at convenience stores, markets, bistros, cafés and restaurants. Check before you leave home that your debit card uses the Interac, Plus or Cirrus systems.

### Traveler's Checks
Traveler's checks are accepted throughout Québec, but if you are traveling to isolated or rural areas, ask in advance to verify their acceptance. Otherwise you should have no real problems cashing American Express, Travelex, Visa or other major brand traveler's checks in either of the city's hotels, restaurants and stores.

### Newspapers
Québec has a wealth of newspapers available at specialty stands. Local papers include *The Montréal Gazette* (daily) and Québec City's weekly *Chronicle-Telegraph* in English. French papers include *Le Devoir*, *La Presse*, *Le Journal de Montréal*, *Le Journal de Québec* and *Le Soleil*.

### Television and Radio
Quebecers have the Canadian networks CBC (government-run), CTV and Global in English, and SRC, TQS, TVA and Téle-Québec in French.

Radio stations are CBC-FM at 93.5 & 88.5 in Montréal and 106.3 in Québec, CJAD 800 AM Talk Radio for English Montréal and INFO 690 AM for French. FM 94.3 CHYZ Radio Laval and CJMF 93.3 FM Classic Rock are active French stations in Québec City and Radio X CHOI at 98.1 FM broadcasts French and English music.

### Tourist Papers and Listings Magazines
Tourisme Montréal publishes the official Tourist Guide each year available at many outlets. Free weeklies list most entertainment activities in both cities: *The Mirror* and *The Hour* (English) and *Voir* & *Ici* (French) are found in stores, restaurants and street boxes.

### Telephones
For cellular/satellite rentals with delivery seven days a week call World Cellular Rentals. To use public telephones, pick up the receiver, dial the number and deposit a flat fee of 25¢ to begin. ✆ *World Cellular Rentals: (1 877) 626 0216.*

### Internet
Internet cafés are located throughout both cities, where for a small fee based on the amount of time you are on line, you can pick up and send e-mails or access information on the web.

Left **Mounted police in Montréal** Right **PharmaPrix pharmacy**

# Security and Health

### Police
All municipal police stations in Québec are connected via the 911 emergency system. To contact police for less urgent business dial (514) 280 2222.

### Fire
Fire stations are also linked to the 911 network in both cities. For non-emergencies call (514) 872 3800 in Montréal; in Québec City check out www.spiq.ca

### Hospitals
Montréal's mega-hospital should be fully operational by 2013, but there are other central hospitals in both cities. ⓢ Montreal: McGill University Health Clinic: 1650 ave Cedar, (514) 937 6011; Children's Hospital: 2300 rue Tupper, (514) 412 4400; Hopital Royal Victoria: 687 ave des Pins Ouest, (514)

842 1231; Le Centre Hospitalier de l'Université de Montréal (French-speaking):3840 rue St-Urbain, (514) 890 8000; • Québec City:Centre Hospitalier Hotel-Dieu de Quebec: 11 côte du Palais, (418) 691 5151

### CLSC
These community health clinics provide neighborhood residents with a range of medical and health-related services and tests. It is possible to obtain immediate medical assistance by walking in to a CLSC. ⓢ CLSC des Faubourgs: 1705 rue Visitation, Montréal, (514) 527 2361 • Cliniques des jeunes Saint-Denis (youth clinic): 1259 rue Sanguinet, Montréal, (514) 844 9333

### Pharmacies
A 24-hour pharmacy in Montréal is located at 5122 chemin de la Côtes-des-Neiges. PharmaPrix is a more central pharmacy, open until midnight, at 901 rue Ste-Catherine Est.

### Disabled Information
Various organizations offer information to disabled travellers. ⓢ Keroul: 4545 ave Pierre-De Coubertin, Montréal; (514) 252 3104; www.keroul.qc.ca • Visites de Montréal; DMC: 2360 rue Notre-Dame Ouest, Suite 203, Montréal; (514) 933 6674; www. visitesdemontreal.com

### Crime
Both cities are relatively crime-free, but the same precautions should apply as for any urban setting. Should you be a victim of crime, contact the police immediately. In Montréal, the Sun Youth Organization provides neighborhood watch teams on foot and bicycle. Crime Stoppers is a telephone service for reporting crime, allowing witness anonymity. ⓢ Sun Youth Organization: 4251 rue St-Urbain; (514) 842 6822 • Crime Stoppers; (514) 393 1133

### Dental Care
Dental services are available at the McCall Clinic in Montréal. For dentists in Québec City, call the number below. ⓢ McCall Dental Clinic:1650 Cedar Ave, 3rd fl.; (514) 934 1934 ext. 47727 • Québec City: (418) 653 5412

### Alternative Health Resources
You can purchase alternative health supplies at Carrefour Santé in Montréal or the Chantal Lacroix Clinic in Québec City. ⓢ Carrefour Santé: 767 rue Rachel Est; (514) 524 7222 • Chantal Lacroix Clinic: (418) 658 2004

### Seasonal Requirements
Travelers visiting in winter must wrap up warm against the deep chill. In summer, bring plenty of suncream.

### Emergency Numbers

**All Emergencies: 911**

**Québec Provincial Police:**
310 4141 (omit the 310 on cell phones)

**Poison Control Centre:**
(1 800) 463 5060

**Disabled advice:**
Keroul; (514) 252 3104

Tele-Aide (514) 935 1101

Left **Avenue Mont-Royal friperies** Right **Place des Arts concert venue**

# Budget Tips

### 1 Tickets and Free Entry

The Montréal Métro subway system offers free travel on New Year's Day, Christmas Day and St-Jean Baptiste (June 24). Tickets for performing arts events can be purchased direct from the venues or via Admission Network. Some clubs offer free admission incentives for the first group of patrons – call the relevant venue for details. ◈ *Admission Network: (514) 790 1245; www.admission.com*

### 2 Free Entertainment

In summer in both cities there are street performers who display their juggling or musical talents free of charge. Shakespeare in the Park entertains crowds around Montréal; check the free weekly newspapers for schedules *(see p108)*. The Vieux-Port areas in the two cities regularly present outdoor concerts, fireworks displays and colorful demonstrations free of charge.

### 3 Discounts and Passes

The best time to obtain discounts and passes is the "shoulder" season, outside the summer or winter tourist rush. To stimulate attendance, businesses will often cut the price of a tour, hotel room or show if you ask ahead of time.

### 4 Cheap Food

Québec is famous for cheap food outlets, from *casse-croûtes* (snack bars) and *patates frites* (French fry) stands, to hot dog and hamburger joints. Ethnic food has boomed with Thai, Vietnamese and Chinese eateries such as Juste Nouilles offering lunch specials for under $5. The rule of thumb in restaurants across all price ranges is to eat your main meal at lunch time to save money.

### 5 Cheap Accommodation

The cheapest accommodations are youth hostels *(see p115)*. The Université du Québec à Montréal has a lavish new *auberge* able to handle singles, doubles or groups *(see p116)*. Local motels are also good value.

### 6 Friperies

Budget-conscious shopping is offered at friperies (secondhand clothiers), selling fashions from every era and style at cheap prices. Rue St-Denis, avenue Mont-Royal, rue Ste-Catherine Est and boulevard St-Laurent are the streets to scout in Montréal.

### 7 Maisons de la Culture

Montréal's secret for frugal entertainment is the Maison de la Culture network, a series of venues offering free or inexpensive performances by artists throughout Montréal districts. The events cover all styles of performing arts, even photographic and art exhibitions.

### 8 Free Times at Museums

Free admission is available to the Musée des Beaux-Arts every day *(see pp20–21)*, and to the Musée d'Art Contemporain de Montréal *(see p66)* on Wednesday evenings from 6pm. On UNESCO's International Museum Day (late May), 28 Montréal museums open their doors free of charge from 9am until 6pm and provide a free shuttle bus service.

### 9 Other Savings

Use toll-free 1-800 reservations systems for accommodations, flights, tours and transportation once in Canada. Do not be afraid to ask for discounts and negotiate deals if you plan paying by cash.

### 10 Club Discounts

If you are a member of an automobile club (AAA), ecotourism network (Sierra Club), hostel organization (HIHOSTEL) or credit card family (Amex/VISA), the chances are you will save a minimum of 10–20 per cent on your car hire, accommodations and travel charges. Check with your club before you leave.

Left **Boulevard St-Laurent restaurant, Montréal** Right **4-star hotel sign**

# TOP 10 Eating and Accommodations Tips

## 1 Types of Dishes and Restaurants

Montréal and Québec City offer travelers a dynamic range of eating choices – diners may choose from a vast selection including delicacies from Afghanistan, Tibet, Algeria, Thailand, the Philippines, Turkey, Poland, San Salvador, Cuba and many other countries. Local favorites include bagels, Montréal smoked meat, and *poutine* (French fries smothered in gravy with cheese).

## 2 Children's Meals

It is common to find children's portions in menu selections – if not, ask your waiter if they would consider offering one to you. Most will gladly comply, not wanting to lose your business. Of course chains such as McDonald's and Burger King are always popular with kids. Some family restaurants even advertise free meals for children under five.

## 3 Tax

The provincial and federal governments impose hefty taxes on top of goods and services in Québec, amounting to 15 per cent. A few merchants include these taxes in their price tags but most do not, so always bear in mind that you will pay more at the cash register. For visitors,

however, federal tax (GST) is refundable on most purchases. You can pick up refund forms at airports, train stations and bus terminals.

## 4 Table d'Hôte Specials

Throughout the Province of Québec, *table d'hôte* menus show up at both lunch and dinner sittings. These menus are fixed-price deals, serving either a soup of the day or salad to start, followed by a choice of principal dishes, then a dessert and coffee or tea. It is the most economical way to dine in Québec.

## 5 Vegetarians

A number of restaurants offer dishes suited to vegetarians, and there are specialty eateries serving only vegetarian fare such as Le Commensal (chain), Govinda Jaya Jaya at 263 rue Duluth, and Kilo Prix at 201 rue St-Viateur in Montréal. Vegetarians may have fewer choices in more rural locations.

## 6 A La Carte Express

This centralized delivery system provides an amazing service, offering access to dozens of restaurants, many of which do not have their own delivery service. They deliver throughout the tourist areas of Montréal. ✆ *A La Carte Express: (514) 933 7000*

## 7 Tipping

In Québec service personnel earn only minimum rates and depend on tips for the larger part of their wages. This does not excuse poor service but is a consideration at gratuity time. Customary tipping in Québec is between 15–20 per cent of the pre-tax total of the bill.

## 8 Smoking Laws

Laws of Québec prohibit smoking in public places, including bars, restaurants and the workplace. Since 2006 the prohibition has been extended and now no smoking is allowed anywhere indoors in Québec.

## 9 Alcohol

Bars and restaurants serve alcohol during hours of operation, usually until 3am. For private consumption, alcohol must be purchased at supermarkets, *dépanneurs* (convenience stores) or, for a wider selection, at *Societé des Alcools du Québec* (SAQ) outlets, which are found in both cities.

## 10 Hotel Ratings

All hotels in Québec are required to have a star classification from the Minister of Tourism. This indicates the facilities available, from basic in 1-star establishments, to luxury features, such as pools and Jacuzzis, in 5-star hotels.

Streetsmart

Left **Ritz-Carlton Montréal** Right **Château Frontenac**

# TOP 10 Luxury Hotels

### 1 Ritz-Carlton Montréal
A longstanding landmark of sophistication and old-world charm, this elegant Neo-Classical structure attracts an élite clientele often seen relaxing with cocktails or English tea in the courtyard garden. Book well in advance. ⬡ 1228 rue Sherbrooke Ouest • Map H1 • (514) 842 4212 • www.ritz carlton.com • Dis. access • $$$$$

### 2 Fairmont Queen Elizabeth Hotel, Montréal
The royalty of Montréal hotels embodies grace and comfort. This was also the location of John Lennon famous "Bed-In" of 1969. ⬡ 900 blvd René-Lévesque Ouest • Map H2 • (514) 861 3511 • www. fairmont.com • Dis. access • $$$$$

### 3 Hôtel le St-James, Montréal
This renovated 1870 building provides visitors with elegant surroundings. Conference facilities, a spa and other touches make one feel pampered. ⬡ 355 rue St-Jacques • Map J3 • (514) 841 3111 • www.hotellestjames.com • Dis. access • $$$$$

### 4 Le Germain, Montréal
This former office build-ing has been transformed into a serene hotel in the midst of all the downtown activity. It is highlighted by excellent food and impeccable service. ⬡ 2050 rue Mansfield • Map H2 • (514) 849 2050 • www. hotelgermain.com • Dis. access • $$$$$

### 5 Hôtel Inter-Continental, Montréal
The InterContinental connects with the Montréal World Trade Center by way of an atrium, where guests and visitors are served a bonanza of shopping and leisure options under one roof. ⬡ 360 rue St-Antoine Ouest • Map J2 • (514) 987 9900 • www.montreal. intercontinental.com • Dis. access • $$$$$

### 6 Hilton Montréal Bonaventure
On top of the 17-story Place Bonaventure con-vention center, the Hilton provides an oasis of comfort and convenience. It has an enticing swim-ming pool and the French cuisine is exquisite at its Le Castillon restaurant. ⬡ 900 rue de la Gauchetière Ouest • Map J2 • (514) 878 2332 • www.hilton montreal.com • Dis. access • $$$$$

### 7 Fairmont Château Frontenac, Québec City
In the center of Vieux-Québec, the Château Frontenac astounds guests with its beauty and luxury. It's decorated as a veritable museum of Canadiana throughout, with a birch-bark canoe and stuffed grizzly bear in the lobby and artifacts on its walls (see p89). ⬡ 1 rue des Carrières • Map L5 • (418) 692 3861 • www.fairmont.com • Dis. access • $$$$$

### 8 Hôtel Château Laurier, Québec City
This friendly hotel faces Parc Georges-V and is within close proximity to Parlement and Parc des Champs-de-Bataille. ⬡ 1220 place George-V Ouest • Map J6 • (418) 522 8108 • www.vieux-quebec.com/ laurier • Dis. access • $$$

### 9 Fairmont le Manoir Richelieu, La Malbaie
This fabulous hotel, dating from 1761, is embellished by a golf course, a casino, and a setting on the St Lawrence River. It frequently attracts US presidents, Hollywood stars and high-rolling gamblers. ⬡ 181 rue Richelieu • Map Q2 • (418) 665 3703 • www.fairmont. com • Dis. access • $$$$$

### 10 Fairmont Tremblant, Mont Tremblant
Golf, spas, adventure activities, boutiques, and restaurants in a village setting. ⬡ 3045 chemin de la Chapelle • Map N5 • (819) 681 7000 • www. fairmont.com • Dis. access • $$$$$

**Note:** Unless otherwise stated, all hotels accept credit cards, have en-suite bathrooms and air conditioning

**Price Categories**

For a standard, double room per night (with breakfast if included), taxes and extra charges.

| | |
|---|---|
| **$** | under $50 |
| **$$** | $50–$100 |
| **$$$** | $100–$150 |
| **$$$$** | $150–$200 |
| **$$$$$** | over $200 |

Above **Le Saint-Sulpice**

# 🔟 Boutique Hotels

## 1 Hôtel Nelligan, Montréal

The Nelligan embraces the concept of boutique hotels, mixing contemporary furnishings with historic elements and designer decor. Features include a roof terrace, European cuisine, a wine cellar and 24-hour concierge service, plus a shuttle bus to downtown. Smart and memorable. ◈ *106 rue St-Paul Ouest • Map K3 • (514) 788 2040 • www.hotelnelligan.com • $$$$$*

## 2 Loews Hôtel Vogue, Montréal

Larger than most boutique hotels with 142 rooms, the Vogue provides guests with a wonderfully central location from which to explore all the sights and the nightlife of the city. It is also the new permanent home for a legend among Montréal's restaurants, Chez George's. ◈ *1425 rue de la Montagne • Map H1 • (514) 285 5555 • www. loewshotels.com • Dis. access • $$$$$*

## 3 Le Saint-Sulpice, Montréal

Literally steps from all the main attractions, yet with an inner courtyard that creates a core of tranquility at the heart of the mayhem. ◈ *414 rue St-Sulpice • Map K3 • (514) 288 1000 • www. lesaintsulpice.com • Dis. access • $$$$$*

## 4 Hôtel St-Paul, Montréal

The exterior of this Beaux-Arts building is deceiving, for inside is minimalist comfort and savvy design. Don't miss the Raw Bar for the best ceviche (raw fish) in town. ◈ *355 rue McGill • Map J3 • (514) 380 2222 • www. hotelstpaul.com • $$$$$*

## 5 Hôtel Place d'Armes, Montréal

This captivating hotel represents the crowning glory of the Antonopoulos family of Québec, who preserved much of Vieux-Montréal's heritage architecture. In the hotel's refined rooms and suites, guests will experience old-world charm and comfort. Features include a rooftop terrace and health club. ◈ *55 rue St-Jacques • Map K2 • (514) 842 1887 • www. hotelplacedarmes.com • $$$$$*

## 6 Château Versailles, Montréal

Myth and legend circulate when speaking of Château Versailles, partly because the four townhouses which it occupies were once home to Montréal's upper crust. Today it welcomes a guest list of performers, artists and writers. Fine dining at La Maîtresse restaurant. ◈ *1659 rue Sherbrooke Ouest • Map A3 • (514) 933 8111 • www.versailleshotels.com • Dis. access • $$$$*

## 7 Le Priori, Québec City

An imaginative little hotel where down-filled duvets and slate showers complement wood-burning fireplaces and full kitchens. ◈ *15 rue Sault-au-Matelot • Map M4 • (418) 692 3992 • www. hotellepriori.com • $$$*

## 8 Hôtel Dominion, Québec City

A mix of heritage elements and contemporary design entice both business and leisure travelers here. Surrounded by attractions, this tiny gem is a real find. ◈ *126 rue St-Pierre • Map M4 • (418) 692 2224 • www.hoteldominion.com • Dis. access • $$$$$*

## 9 Auberge St-Antoine, Québec City

This former warehouse, carefully restored, offers one-of-a-kind decor, a waterfront setting and amenities such as modem outlets. ◈ *8 rue St-Antoine • Map M4 • (418) 692 2211 • www. saint-antoine.com • $$$$*

## 10 Manoir le Tricorne, North Hatley

The perfect intimate location overlooking Lake Massawippi and offering 90 acres of land. Every effort is made to accommodate travelers' needs. ◈ *50 chemin Gosselin • Map Q6 • (819) 842 4522 • www.manoirletricorne. com • Dis. access • $$$$*

Left **Armor Manoir Sherbrooke** Right **Hôtel Terrasse Dufferin**

# TOP 10 Mid-Range and Chain Hotels

### 1 Hôtel de l'Institut, Montréal
This hotel doubles as an educational training center for students in the tourism industry. Trainees are at your service in both the hotel and the restaurant. Located downtown, near the Plateau and the Latin Quarter, overlooking Square St-Louis. Breakfast included. ⊗ *3535 rue St-Denis • Map E3 • (514) 282 5181 • www.ithq.qc.ca/hotel • Dis. access • $$$*

### 2 Best Western Montréal Airport Hotel
Along the commercial thoroughfare from Montréal International Airport Dorval, visitors are shuttled here free of charge around the clock. Standard hotel comforts and an inexpensive option for travelers on a budget. ⊗ *13000 chemin Côte-de-Liesse, Dorval • Free shuttle bus • (514) 631 4811 • www.bestwestern.com • Dis. access • $$$*

### 3 Armor Manoir Sherbrooke, Montréal
A heritage exterior gives way to plush accommodations inside. Friendly staff, proud of their *manoir*, offer a 24-hour reception, suites with whirlpools, and Internet facilities. ⊗ *157 rue Sherbrooke Est • Map D3 • (514) 845 0915 • www.armormanoir.com • $$$*

### 4 Montréal Hyatt Regency
This is the hotel chosen by the International Jazz Festival of Montréal as the host site for their Midnight Jam Sessions. The hotel has an airy, cosmopolitan energy throughout, the staff are professional and the rooms top notch. ⊗ *1255 rue Jeanne Mance • Map D1 • (514) 285-1450 • http://montreal.hyatt.com • Dis. access • $$$$*

### 5 Sofitel, Montréal
With access to galleries, museums, shopping and nightlife, the Sofitel stands as a welcome luxury chain addition to the city's underlying shortage of hotel rooms. Every frill and service is available. Dining excellence is on-site at Le Renoir restaurant. ⊗ *1155 rue Sherbrooke Ouest, Montréal • Map B3 • (514) 285 9000 • www.sofitel.com • Dis. access • $$$$$*

### 6 Le Château de Pierre, Québec City
A million-dollar location attracts visitors to this charming hotel. Rooms are decorated in the style of the British Colonial era and maintain an air of refinement. Rooms have views of the St Lawrence River or the garden. ⊗ *17 ave Ste-Geneviève • Map L5 • (418) 694 0429 • www.chateaudepierre.com • $$$*

### 7 Hôtel Terrasse Dufferin, Québec City
Spectacular views of the Château Frontenac and St Lawrence River make this a memorable stay. Rooms are well appointed with amenities such as kitchenettes and balconies. ⊗ *6 place de la Terrasse-Dufferin • Map L5 • (418) 694-9472 • www.terrasse-dufferin.com • $$$*

### 8 Loews le Concorde, Québec City
With over 400 rooms, the hotel is capped by the L'Astral restaurant with a 360-degree revolving view. ⊗ *1225 place Montcalm • Map J6 • (418) 647 2222 • www.loewshotels.com • Dis. access • $$$$$*

### 9 Hôtel Manoir Victoria, Québec City
Mahogany desks, wood panelling and a magnificent hall welcome guests to this historic building. Pool, parking and restaurant. ⊗ *44 côte du Palais • Map K4 • (418) 692 1030 • www.manoir-victoria.com • Dis. access • $$$$*

### 10 Hilton Québec, Québec City
The Hilton offers 577 sumptuous rooms, a great view and vicinity to Place Québec shopping. ⊗ *1100 blvd René-Lévesque Est • (418) 647 2411 • www.hilton.com • Dis. access • $$$$$*

**Note:** *Unless otherwise stated, all hotels accept credit cards, have en-suite bathrooms and air conditioning*

Above Le Gîte du Plateau Mont-Royal

| Price Categories | | |
|---|---|---|
| For a standard, double room per night (with breakfast if included), taxes and extra charges. | **$** under $50<br>**$$** $50–$100<br>**$$$** $100–$150<br>**$$$$** $150–$200<br>**$$$$$** over $200 | |

# 🔟 Budget Hotels and Hostels

## 1 HI Youth Hostel, Montréal
Rates vary at this Montréal hostelling institution that has been in operation for over 70 years. It offers affordable single rooms and dorms with up to six beds. Located in the heart of downtown. ✪ 103 rue Mackay • Map G1 • (514) 843 3317 • www. hostellingmontreal.com • $–$$

## 2 YWCA, Montréal
Y des Femmes (Y for women) has become a very popular place since the larger YMCA closed its 330 rooms. This hotel has 64 comfortable rooms in a choice of shared bathroom facilities or en-suite. The ambiance is friendly and the location makes it possible to walk to major attractions and restaurants in the downtown core. Cable TV, indoor pool, 24-hour reception, laundry and health center. ✪ 1355 blvd René-Lévesque Ouest • Map H2 • (514) 866 9941 • www.ydesfemmesmtl.org • $$$

## 3 Le Gîte du Plateau Mont-Royal, Montréal
These longstay studios are located in the heart of Le Plateau, with access to boulevard Saint-Laurent and Vieux-Montréal. ✪ 185 rue Sherbrooke Est • Map D3 • (514) 284 1276 • www. hostelmontreal.com • $

## 4 Auberge de Jeunesse de Montréal
The Auberge de Jeunesse has been offering travelers downtown lodging for over 30 years and prides itself on continuing to provide an inexpensive alternative for individuals, families and groups. Educational, cultural and environmental tours offered. Try to book a week before arrival. ✪ 1030 rue Mackay • Map G2 • (514) 843 3317 • www. hostellingmontreal.com • Dis. access • $$

## 5 Auberge Alternative de Vieux-Montréal
An independant hostel in Vieux-Montréal. No-curfew policy, free Internet access, kitchen facilities, small and large dormitories and private accommodations. ✪ 358 rue St-Pierre • Map K3 • (514) 282 8069 • www. auberge-alternative.qc.ca • No credit cards • $

## 6 Auberge Saint-Louis, Québec City
Well-kept rooms with cable TV and a shared or en-suite bathroom make this Vieux Québec hotel a real find. Within walking distance to most sights, clubs and restaurants. Ask about packages that include dinner in the price. ✪ 48 rue St-Louis • Map L5 • (418) 692 2424 • www.aubergestlouis.ca • $$

## 7 La Belle Planete Downtown Québec Hostel, Québec City
Close to the train and bus stations and the antiques shops of rue St-Paul, this clean hostel has 24-hour showers and lockers available in dorms with eight to ten beds. An inviting and convenient option. ✪ 386 rue du Pont • Map J4 • (418) 264 4615 • www. planetebackpackers.com • $

## 8 Centre International de Séjours de Québec, Québec City
Single, double or dormitory choices are offered, with fully equipped kitchen, games room and Internet available. ✪ 19 rue Ste-Ursule • Map K5 • (418) 694 0755 • www. cisq.org • Dis. access • $$

## 9 Auberge de la Paix, Québec City
This hip hostel has 60 beds with between two to eight travelers to a room. Breakfast included. ✪ 31 rue Couillard • Map L4 • (418) 694 0735 • www. aubergedelapaix.com • $

## 10 Auberge de Jeunesse le P'tit Bonheur, Ile d'Orléans
Horse riding and cross-country skiing can be enjoyed while staying here. ✪ 186 côte Lafleur, St-Jean • Map P3 • (418) 829 2588 • www.leptit bonheur.qc.ca • Dis. access • $$

Left **Auberge Sauvignon** Right **Auberge Comte de Watel**

# 🔟 Auberges

### 1 Auberge des Passants du Sans-Soucy, Montréal
At this 18th-century auberge the hosts spoil you with flowers, fine art, brass beds and a warm fireplace, a full gourmet breakfast and a Jacuzzi. ⬡ *171 St-Paul Ouest • Map K3 • (514) 842 2634 • www.lesanssoucy. com • $$$*

### 2 Auberge le Jardin d'Antoine, Montréal
This Quartier Latin hotel delivers a prime historic location, friendly bilingual staff, modern accommodations, a charming breakfast salon and parking. ⬡ *2024 rue St-Denis • Map L1 • (514) 843 4506 • www. aubergelejardindantoine. com • $$$*

### 3 Auberge de la Fontaine, Montréal
Rooms perched overlooking Parc Lafontaine, colorful, contemporary furnishings in all 21 soundproof rooms and a 24-hour reception desk make it easy to see why this auberge has a loyal clientele. ⬡ *1301 rue Rachel Est • Map E2 • (514) 597 0166 • www. aubergedelafontaine.com • Dis. access • $$$$$*

### 4 Hostellerie Pierre du Calvet 1725, Montréal
Four-poster beds, heavy window sashes and ornate furnishings cast visitors back to the early

1700s. Beamed ceilings, family heirlooms and rich French cuisine complete the package. Lovely breakfast atrium and lounge for cocktails. ⬡ *405 rue Bonsecours • Map L3 • (514) 282 1725 • www.pierreducalvet.ca • $$$$$*

### 5 Auberge St-Louis, Québec City
Value-conscious travelers will welcome this Vieux-Québec economy option with its colorful decor. From here it is possible to stroll to most of the major sights and eateries in the area. ⬡ *48 rue St-Louis • Map L5 • (418) 692 2424 • www. aubergestlouis.ca • $$*

### 6 Auberge Ripplecove, Ayer's Cliff
Holders of the coveted Five Star status from the Québec Tourism authorities, this auberge garners praise from all corners for its romantic rooms, spectacular setting overlooking Lake Massawippi and Four Diamond dining excellence. ⬡ *700 rue Ripplecove • Map Q6 • (819) 838 4296 • www. ripplecove.com • Dis. access • $$$$$*

### 7 Auberge Sauvignon, Mont-Tremblant
Located away from the crowds at the resort, this tranquil hostelry exudes a confident elegance and

host Patrick delights in serving guests tantalizing seafood specialties or hearty meat options. ⬡ *2723 chemin Principal off Rte 327 • Map N5 • (819) 425 5466 • www. aubergesauvignon.com • Dis. access • $$$$*

### 8 Auberge Comte de Watel, Ste-Agathe-des-Monts
A remarkable auberge with views of Lac des Sables. A complete range of equipment can be rented from the hotel, including fishing boats, kayaks, canoes, sailboats, snowmobiles and quad bikes. ⬡ *250 rue St-Venant • Map N5 • (819) 326 7016 • www.watel.ca • Dis. access • $$$$*

### 9 Manoir Hovey, North Hatley
This early 20th-century inn with white columns, palatial grounds and antique-filled rooms overlooks Lake Massawippi. ⬡ *575 chemin Hovey • Map Q6 • (819) 842 2421 • www.manoirhovey.com • Dis. access • $$$$$*

### 🔟 Auberge L'Etoile sur le Lac
On the shores of Lac Memphrémagog, this is both an inn and a restaurant offering luxury accommodation and food with a Mediterranean flavor. ⬡ *1200 rue Principale Ouest, Magog • Map Q6 • (819) 843 6521 • www.etoile-sur-le-lac.com • Dis. access • $$$$$*

**Note:** *Unless otherwise stated, all hotels accept credit cards, have en-suite bathrooms and air conditioning*

**Price Categories**

For a standard, double room per night (with breakfast if included), taxes and extra charges.

| | |
|---|---|
| **$** | under $50 |
| **$$** | $50–$100 |
| **$$$** | $100–$150 |
| **$$$$** | $150–$200 |
| **$$$$$** | over $200 |

Above **Auberge le Canard Huppé**

# 🔟 Gîtes and Champêtres

### 1 Bed-and-Breakfast Downtown Network, Montréal

Amassing 80 different host homes, organizers Bob and Mariko arrange rooms for travelers in the central neighborhoods of Montréal near major attractions, shopping, restaurants and transportation hubs. ⌾ *3458 ave Laval • Map D2 • (514) 289 9749 • www. bbmontreal.qc.ca • $$$*

### 2 Les Bonbons 67, Montréal

Located a stone's throw away from the attractions of the Quartier Latin and Gay Village, this B&B housed in a restored 19th-century house offers excellent rates. The owners' beagle, Albert, will be the first to welcome you. ⌾ *1628 rue St-Christophe • Map M1 • (514) 906 1523 • www. lesbonbons67.com • $$*

### 3 Petite Auberge Les Bons Matins, Montréal

This bohemian inn provides friendly service, freshly cooked gourmet breakfasts, and uniquely decorated rooms. The building also houses an art gallery. ⌾ *1401 rue Argyle • Map C4 • (514) 931 9167 • www.bons matins.com • $$$*

### 4 Auberge aux Deux Lions, Québec City

Close to all the major attractions, this B&B boasts affordable but charming lodgings in a century-old building. There are also three family suites. ⌾ *25 blvd René-Lévesque Est • (418) 780 8100 • www.auberge auxdeuxlions.com • $$$*

### 5 La Marquise de Bassano, Québec City

La Marquise de Bassano is located in a quiet street in the heart of Old Québec. Its 19th-century decor, stained glass and high ceilings – even the original bells used to summon the servants! – mark this as an authentic legacy of Québec's rich wealth history. ⌾ *15 rue des Grisons • Map L5 • (418) 692 0316 • www.marquise debassano.com • $$$*

### 6 Hostellerie Rive Gauche, Beloeil

Located south of Montréal, this modern *hostellerie* overlooks the grandeur of the Richelieu River and the rising Mont St-Hilaire. Seventeen rooms and five suites with whirlpool. ⌾ *1810 blvd Richelieu • Map P6 • (450) 467 4477 • www.hostellerierivegauche. com • $$$$*

### 7 Auberge le Canard Huppé, Ile d'Orléans

Islanders recommend this shoreside inn and villas whenever guests visit, partly due to the relaxed and tasteful ambiance but equally because of the gastronomic delights available. ⌾ *2198 chemin Royal, Saint-Laurent • Map P3 • (418) 828 2292 • www. canard-huppe.com • Dis. access • $$$*

### 8 Auberge la Camarine, Beaupré

Situated at the foot of Mont-Ste-Anne's ski resort and hugging the banks of the Rivière Ste-Anne, Auberge La Camarine serves ample portions of pleasure and relaxation. There are 29 rooms and two suites. ⌾ *10947 blvd Ste-Anne • Map P3 • (418) 827 5703 • www.camarine.com • $$$*

### 9 Auberge Lakeview Inn, Knowlton

This waterfront antique-filled Victorian domain near Lac Brome has 29 rooms, four studios and four conference rooms. ⌾ *50 rue Victoria • Map Q6 • (450) 243 6183 • www. aubergelakeviewinn.com • Dis. access • $$$$$*

### 10 Auberge des Gallant, Rigaud

A year-round sanctuary, where deer roam the local landscape at dawn and dusk. The comfortable rooms include all modern amenities. ⌾ *1171 chemin St-Henri, Sainte-Marthe • Map N6 • (450) 459 4241 • www. gallant.qc.ca • Dis. access • $$$$*

> *Gîte is the local French term for bed-and-breakfast; champêtres are country inns.*

117

# General Index

# Acknowledgements

**Main Contributor**

Gregory B. Gallagher is a freelance writer, editor, musician and historian based in his native Montréal. His travel articles appear in *The Montréal Gazette*, and he is currently Food, Travel and Special Events Editor for *Trendmaker Magazine*.

Produced by Sargasso Media Ltd, London

**Editorial Director** Zoë Ross
**Art Editor** Clare Thorpe
**Picture Research** Helen Stallion
**Proofreader** Stewart J Wild
**Editorial Assistance** Jacqueline To

**Main Photographer**
Demetrio Carrasco
**Additional Photographers**
Gregory B. Gallagher, Alan Keohane
**Illustrator** chrisorr.com

FOR DORLING KINDERSLEY
**Publisher** Douglas Amrine
**Publishing Managers** Jane Ewart, Kathryn Lane
**Senior Cartographic Editor**
Casper Morris
**DTP** Jason Little
**Production** Shane Higgins
**Maps** Martin Darlison & Tom Coulson, Encompass Graphics Ltd
**Revisions** Tessa Bindloss, Eric and Katharine Fletcher, Rhiannon Furbear, Patrick Lejtenyi, Carly Madden, Nicola Malone, Kate Molan, Helen Partington, Sands Publishing Solutions

**Picture Credits**

t-top; tc-top centre; tr-top right; cla-centre left above; ca-centre above; cra-centre right above; cl-centre left; c-centre; cr-centre right; clb-centre left below; cb-centre below; crb-centre right below; bl-below left; bc-below centre; br-below right.

Every effort has been made to trace the copyright holders, and we apologize in advance for any unintentional omissions. We would be pleased to insert the appropriate acknowledgements in any subsequent edition of this publication.

The publishers would like to thank the following individuals, companies, and picture libraries for permission to reproduce their photographs:

ARCHIVES NATIONALES DU QUÉBEC À QUÉBEC: 38b; AUBERGE RESTAURANT LE CANARD HUPPÉ: 117tl; AUBERGE SAUVIGNON: 116tl; AUBERGE WATEL: 116tr.

BARRACA RHUMERIE & TAPAS: 78tl; BASILIQUE-SAINTE-ANNE-DE-BEAUPRÉ: 3 bl, 26–27.

CARNAVAL DE QUÉBEC: 44tr; CIRQUE DU SOLEIL À MONTRÉAL: Benoit Camirand 39b; Al Saib 57r; CORBIS: 16tl, 32tl, 32tr, 32b, 33cr, 36tr, 36b, 38tl, 38tr, 39tl, 43t, 46tr, 47, 50tr, 69tr, 76b, 89t, 92tr, 93tr, 105tr, 107tr.

DAGOBERT NIGHT-CLUB: 97tr.

FAIRMONT LE CHATEAU FRONTENAC: 99tl; FESTIVAL INTERNATIONAL DE JAZZ DE MONTRÉAL: 42tr; FESTIVAL MONTRÉAL EN LUMIÈRE: 42b; WINSTON FRASER: 30 tl, 44b, 84tl, 84tr.

GRAND PRIX DE MONTRÉAL: 42 tl, 49r.

JARDIN BOTANIQUE ET INSECTARIUM DE MONTRÉAL: 15t, 17b, 46tl.

LES PRODUCTIONS TESSIMA LTÉE: 31t, 44tl, 44c, 48 tr, 48b, 49tl, 83r, 101t; Yves Tessier 2 tr.

MAUDSTAIRS HOLDINGS INC.: 62tl; MAURICE NIGHT CLUB: 50tl; MUSÉE DE LA CIVILISATION DE QUÉBEC: Jacques Lessard 24–25, 25b; MUSÉE DES BEAUX-ARTS DE MONTRÉAL: Photo Marilyn Aitken, Rembrandt, *Portrait d'une jeune femme*, 20c; Photo Denis Farley, Jean-Paul Riopelle *La Roué*, © ADAGP, Paris and DACS, London 2003, 21t; MUSÉE POINTE-À-CALLIÈRE: 6cr, 18tl, 18b, /Normand Rajotte 19cr.

ORATOIRE ST-JOSEPH: 11b.

PARC OLYMPIQUE: 14-15; PICTURES COLOUR LIBRARY: 28–29; PUBLI-PHOTO: 22–23, 30c, 30b, 60–61, 70–71, 80tl, 80c, 82, 86tl, 86tr.

SALON DU THÉ COEUR SOLEIL: 85.

TOURISME MONTRÉAL: 46b, 48tl; TOURISME QUÉBEC: 3br, 45, 100;

TREMBLANT: 7, 30–31, 81.

UPSTAIRS AT JAZZ: 51t.

LE VIEUX SAINT-GABRIEL: 62tr.

All other images are © Dorling Kindersley. For further information see *www.dkimages.com*

DK publishes a wide range of guidebooks, including over 70 in this Eyewitness Top Ten series and more than 100 in the award-winning Eyewitness Travel Guide series. To see our complete range of guides, phrasebooks and maps, visit us at **www.dk.com**

## Dorling Kindersley Special Editions

Dorling Kindersley books can be purchased in bulk quantities at discounted prices for use in promotions or as premiums. We are also able to offer special editions and personalized jackets, corporate imprints, and excerpts from all of our books, tailored specifically to meet your own needs.

To find out more, please contact: (in the United Kingdom) – travelspecialsales@uk. dk.com or Special Sales, Dorling Kindersley Limited, 80 Strand, London WC2R 0RL; (in the United States) – Special Markets Department, DK Publishing, 375 Hudson Street, New York, New York 10014.

# Phrase Book

## In Emergency

| | | |
|---|---|---|
| Help! | **Au secours!** | oh sekoor |
| Stop! | **Arrêtez!** | aret-ay |
| Call a doctor! | **Appelez un médecin!** | apuh-lay uñ medsañ |
| Call an ambulance! | **Appelez une ambulance!** | apuh-lay oon oñboo-loñs |
| Call the police! | **Appelez la police!** | apuh-lay lah poh-lees |
| Call the fire department! | **Appelez les pompiers!** | apuh-lay leh poñ-peeyay |

## Communication Essentials

| | | |
|---|---|---|
| Yes/No | **Oui/ Non** | wee/noñ |
| Please | **S'il vous plaît** | seel voo play |
| Thank you | **Merci** | mer-see |
| Excuse me | **Excusez-moi** | exkoo-zay mwah |
| Hello | **Bonjour** | boñzhoor |
| Goodbye | **Au revoir** | oh ruh-vwar |
| Good night | **Bonsoir** | boñ-swar |
| What? | **Quel, quelle?** | kel, kel |
| When? | **Quand?** | koñ |
| Why? | **Pourquoi?** | poor-kwah |
| Where? | **Où?** | oo |

## Useful Phrases

| | | |
|---|---|---|
| How are you? | **Comment allez-vous?** | kom-moñ talay voo |
| Very well, | **Très bien,** | treh byañ |
| Pleased to meet you. | **Enchanté de faire votre connaissance** | oñshoñ-tay duh fehr votr kon-ay-sans |
| Where is/are…? | **Où est/sont…?** | oo ay/soñ |
| Which way to…? | **Quelle est la direction pour…?** | kel ay lah deer-ek-syoñ poor |
| Do you speak English? | **Parlez-vous anglais?** | par-lay voo oñg-lay |
| I don't understand. | **Je ne comprends pas.** | zhuh nuh kom-proñ pah |
| I'm sorry. | **Excusez-moi** | exkoo-zay mwah |

## Useful Words

| | | |
|---|---|---|
| big | **grand** | groñ |
| small | **petit** | puh-tee |
| hot | **chaud** | show |
| cold | **froid** | frwah |
| good | **bon** | boñ |
| bad | **mauvais** | moh-veh |
| open | **ouvert** | oo-ver |
| closed | **fermé** | fer-meh |
| left | **gauche** | gohsh |
| right | **droite** | drwaht |
| straight ahead | **tout droit** | too drwah |
| entrance | **l'entrée** | l'on-tray |
| exit | **la sortie** | sor-tee |

## Shopping

| | | |
|---|---|---|
| How much does this cost? | **C'est combien s'il vous plaît?** | say kom-byañ seel voo play |
| I would like… | **je voudrais…** | zhuh voo-dray |
| Do you have? | **Est-ce que vous avez?** | es-kuh voo zavay |
| Do you take credit cards? | **Est-ce que vous acceptez les cartes de crédit?** | es-kuh voo zaksept-ay leh kart duh krehdee |
| What time do you open? | **A quelle heure vous êtes ouvert?** | ah kel urr voo zet oo-ver |
| What time do you close? | **A quelle heure vous êtes fermé?** | ah kel urr voo zet fer-may |
| This one. | **Celui-ci.** | suhl-wee-see |
| That one. | **Celui-là** | suhl-wee-lah |
| expensive | **cher** | shehr |
| cheap | **pas cher, bon marché** | pah shehr, boñ mar-shay |
| size, clothes | **la taille** | tye |
| size, shoes | **la pointure** | pwañ-tur |
| white | **blanc** | bloñ |
| black | **noir** | nwahr |
| red | **rouge** | roozh |
| yellow | **jaune** | zhohwn |
| green | **vert** | vehr |
| blue | **bleu** | bluh |

## Types of Shop

| | | |
|---|---|---|
| antique store | **le magasin d'antiquités** | maga-zañ d'oñteekee-tay |
| bakery | **la boulangerie** | booloñ-zhuree |
| bank | **la banque** | boñk |
| bookstore | **la librairie** | lee-brehree |
| cake shop | **la pâtisserie** | patee-sree |
| cheese shop | **la fromagerie** | fromazh-ree |
| chemist | **la pharmacie** | farmah-see |
| convenience store | **le dépanneur** | deh-pan-urr |
| department store | **le grand magasin** | groñ maga-zañ |
| delicatessen | **la charcuterie** | sharkoot-ree |
| gift shop | **le magasin de cadeaux** | maga-zañ duh kadoh |
| fruit and vegetable store | **le marchand de légumes** | mar-shoñ duh lay-goom |
| grocery store | **l'alimentation** | alee-moñta-syoñ |
| market | **le marché** | marsh-ay |
| newsstand | **le magasin de journaux** | maga-zañ duh zhoor-no |
| post office | **la poste, le bureau de poste** | pohst, booroh duh pohst |
| supermarket | **le supermarché** | soo pehr-marshay |
| smoke shop | **la tabacie** | tabah-see |
| travel agent | **l'agence de voyages** | l'azhoñs duh vwayazh |

## Sightseeing

| | | |
|---|---|---|
| abbey | **l'abbaye** | l'abay-ee |
| art gallery | **la galerie d'art** | galer-ree dart |
| bus station | **la gare d'autobus** | gahr door-to-boos |
| cathedral | **la cathédrale** | katay-dral |
| church | **l'église** | l'aygleez |
| garden | **le jardin** | zhar-dañ |
| library | **la bibliothèque** | beebleeo-tek |
| museum | **le musée** | moo-zay |
| train station | **la gare** | gahr |
| tourist information office | **le bureau d'information** | booroh duh infor-mah-syoñ, |
| town hall | **l'hôtel de ville** | l'ohtel duh veel |

## Staying in a Hotel

| | | |
|---|---|---|
| Do you have a vacant room? | **Est-ce que vous avez une chambre?** | es-kuh voo-zavay oon shambr |
| double room, with double bed | **la chambre pour deux** | shambr poor duh |

Phrase Book

|  |  |  | milk | le lait | leh |
|---|---|---|---|---|---|
| twin room | personnes, avec un grand lit | pehr-son avek un gronñ lee | mineral water | l'eau minérale | l'oh meeney-ral |
| | la chambre à deux lits | shambr ah duh lee | oil | l'huile | l'weel |
| single room | la chambre pour une personne | shambr poor oon pehr-son | onions | les oignons | leh zonyoñ |
| | | | fresh orange juice | jus d'orange frais | zhu d'oroñzh fray |
| room with a bath, shower | la chambre avec salle de bains, une douche | shambr avek sal duh bañ, oon doosh | fresh lemon juice | jus de citron frais | zhu de see-troñ fray |
| I have a reservation. | J'ai fait une réservation. | zhay fay oon rayzehrva-syoñ | pepper | le poivre | pwavr |
| | | | pork | le porc | por |
| | | | potatoes | pommes de terre | pom-duh tehr |

**Eating Out**

| | | | rice | le riz | ree |
|---|---|---|---|---|---|
| Have you got a table? | Avez-vous une table de libre? | avay-voo oon tahbl duh leebr | roast | rôti | row-tee |
| I want to reserve a table. | Je voudrais réserver une table. | zhuh voo-dray rayzehr-vay oon tahbl | salt | le sel | sel |
| | | | sausage, fresh | la saucisse | sohsees |
| The bill please. | L'addition s'il vous plaît. | l'adee-syoñ seel voo play | seafood | les fruits de mer | frwee duh mer |
| Waitress/ waiter | Madame, Mademoiselle/ Monsieur | mah-dam, mah-demwahzel/ muh-syuh | snails | les escargots | leh zes-kar-goh |
| | | | soup | la soupe, le potage | soop, poh-tazh |
| menu | le menu, la carte | men-oo, kart | steak | le bifteck | beef-tek, stek |
| fixed-price menu | la table d'hôte | tahb-luh dote | sugar | le sucre | sookr |
| | | | tea | le thé | tay |
| cover charge | le couvert | koo-vehr | vegetables | les légumes | lay-goom |
| wine list | la carte des vins | kart-deh vañ | vinegar | le vinaigre | veenaygr |
| glass | le verre | vehr | water | l'eau | l'oh |
| bottle | la bouteille | boo-tay | red wine | le vin rouge | vañ roozh |
| knife | le couteau | koo-toh | white wine | le vin blanc | vañ bloñ |
| fork | la fourchette | for-shet | | | |

**Numbers**

| spoon | la cuillère | kwee-yehr | 0 | zéro | zeh-roh |
|---|---|---|---|---|---|
| breakfast | le petit déjeuner | puh-tee deh-zhuh-nay | 1 | un, une | uñ, oon |
| lunch | le déjeuner | deh-zhuh-nay | 2 | deux | duh |
| dinner | le dîner | dee-nay | 3 | trois | trwah |
| main course | le plat principal | plah prañsee-pal | 4 | quatre | katr |
| | | | 5 | cinq | sañk |
| appetizer, first course | l'entrée, les hors d'oeuvre | l'oñ-tray, or-duhvr | 6 | six | sees |
| | | | 7 | sept | set |
| dish of the day | le plat du jour | plah doo zhoor | 8 | huit | weet |
| wine bar | le bar à vin | bar ah vañ | 9 | neuf | nerf |
| café | le café | ka-fay | 10 | dix | dees |
| | | | 11 | onze | oñz |

**Menu Decoder**

| | | | 12 | douze | dooz |
|---|---|---|---|---|---|
| baked | cuit au four | kweet oh foor | 13 | treize | trehz |
| beef | le boeuf | buhf | 14 | quatorze | katorz |
| beer | la bière | bee-yehr | 15 | quinze | kañz |
| boiled | bouilli | boo-yee | 16 | seize | sehz |
| bread | le pain | pan | 17 | dix-sept | dees-set |
| butter | le beurre | burr | 18 | dix-huit | dees-weet |
| cake | le gâteau | gah-toh | 19 | dix-neuf | dees-nerf |
| cheese | le fromage | from-azh | 20 | vingt | vañ |
| chicken | le poulet | poo-lay | 30 | trente | tront |
| chips | les frites | freet | 40 | quarante | karoñt |
| chocolate | le chocolat | shoko-lah | 50 | cinquante | sañkoñt |
| coffee | le café | kah-fay | 60 | soixante | swasoñt |
| dessert | le dessert | deh-ser | 70 | soixante-dix | swasoñt-dees |
| egg | l'oeuf | l'uf | 80 | quatre-vingts | katr-vañ |
| fish | le poisson | pwah-ssoñ | 90 | quatre-vingt-dix | katr-vañ-dees |
| fresh fruit | les fruits frais | frwee freh | 100 | cent | soñ |
| garlic | l'ail | l'eye | 1,000 | mille | meel |
| grilled | grillé | gree-yay | | | |

**Time**

| ham | le jambon | zhoñ-boñ | one minute | une minute | oon mee-noot |
|---|---|---|---|---|---|
| ice cream | la crème glacée | crem glas-ay | one hour | une heure | oon urr |
| ice cubes | les glaçons | glas-oñ | half an hour | une demi-heure | urr duh-me urr |
| lamb | l'agneau | l'anyoh | one day | un jour | urr zhorr |
| lemon | le citron | see-troñ | Monday | lundi | luñ-dee |
| meat | la viande | vee-yand | Tuesday | mardi | mar-dee |
| | | | Wednesday | mercredi | mehrkruh-dee |
| | | | Thursday | jeudi | zhuh-dee |
| | | | Friday | vendredi | voñdruh-dee |
| | | | Saturday | samedi | sam-dee |
| | | | Sunday | dimanche | dee-moñsh |

# Selected Street Index

128